BEYOND OFFENDING BEHAVIOUR

DEDICATION

For Nigel Henery, in whose own practice and teaching the themes of this book are so well reflected.

Beyond Offending Behaviour

edited by
Mark Drakeford
Maurice Vanstone

Published by
Arena
Ashgate Publishing Limited
Gower House
Croft Road
Aldershot
Hants GU11 3HR
England

Ashgate Publishing Company
Old Post Road
Brookfield
Vermont 05036
USA

British Library Cataloguing in Publication Data

Beyond Offending Behaviour
   I. Drakeford, Mark II. Vanstone, Maurice
   364. 630941

Library of Congress Catalog Card Number: 95-81228

ISBN 1 85742 239 2 (paperback)
ISBN 1 85742 238 4 (hardback)

Typeset in Palatino by Poole Typesetting and printed in Great Britain by Hartnolls Ltd, Bodmin.

Contents

Preface and acknowledgements

These are troubled times for the Probation Service and, in some important ways, this book has been born out of these troubles. The chapters and commentaries which follow attempt to make a convincing case for a particular form of practice which, we argue, has received insufficient attention in recent years.

Yet, most importantly, this is not a pessimistic book. It does not suggest that there was some golden age for probation which has since gone badly wrong. Many of the things which contemporary probation officers carry out daily are improvements on previous practice. Increasingly, there is a greater concern with how people are helped and whether the intended outcomes of interventions are achieved effectively. Where we identify a real deficit – in the attention which the Service now provides to the social context of people's lives – at least half of the book is devoted to present-day examples of good practice where that deficit is being actively addressed. As editors, our concern has been to suggest ways in which those examples might be built upon and made a more central part of policy-making and practice.

Each chapter of this book begins with a survey which sets out the state of key social systems upon which we all rely, and then examines in detail the impact of these systems on the lives of people who appear before the Courts. With that survey we link a Commentary which illustrates ways in which the negative impact of these systems can be productively addressed by social welfare services. The general point we make – that changes in people's lives can best be brought about when the circumstances in which they live are also changed for the better – applies to all forms of social work, not simply within the criminal justice system.

Our optimism that this sort of practice can still be achieved has been increased and strengthened by the process of preparing the Commentary sections. The examples of work contained there were obtained from a series of sources. First, we drew upon the significant literature through which Probation Service practitioners tell one another about the work in which they are engaged – even if our experience suggests that they do not speak often enough or loud enough about its nature and quality. Second, we have drawn upon our own contacts in South Wales. The number of examples which we have been able to include from this limited geographical area is an illustration, we believe, of the continuing vitality of this way of working. Finally, through a series of specific contacts with individuals and projects we have obtained an insight into work which is currently in progress. Together these sources provide templates for the policy and practice direction which forms the argument of this book.

As editors, our first acknowledgements are owed to our contributors whose careful cooperation has made our task an easier one than would otherwise have been, and without whom, of course, this book would not have been produced. As well as those whose names appear directly in the text, there are a whole series of friends and colleagues in the field who have responded readily to our requests for ideas and information. Their contributions appear in our own Commentary sections and are, we hope, a tribute to the continuing commitment and ingenuity of practising probation officers, and others still determined to make a positive impact upon the social circumstances which contribute to crime and dominate the lives of those caught up in it.

Particular thanks go to Rob Thomas who read an early draft and to Jo Campling from whose advice and assistance we benefited. Her continued interest, and that of staff at Arena, has seen us through to completion.

Mark Drakeford and Maurice Vanstone

Contributors

Jon Arnold is a former probation officer and is now Lecturer in Social Studies at the University of Exeter, where he retains a major responsibility for probation training.

Iain Crow was head of research at NACRO (the National Association for the Care and Resettlement of Offenders) from 1974–1989. During that time he was responsible for a number of studies relating to unemployed offenders, including employment and training schemes for offenders, employment training in Young Offender Institutions, and the effects of unemployment on the sentencing of offenders. Since 1989 he has been teaching and researching at the Centre for Criminological and Legal Research at the University of Sheffield.

Mark Drakeford is Lecturer in Social Policy and Applied Social Studies at University College, Swansea. He is a former probation officer and Barnardos project leader and has published many articles in the areas of criminal justice and poverty.

Bill Jordan is the author of many texts on social policy and social work. He is Reader in Social Studies at the University of Exeter and currently holds the Chair of European Social Policy at the University of Bratislava.

Joan Orme is Senior Lecturer in Social Work Studies at the University of Southampton. Before joining the university, she was a probation officer and has maintained involvement in, and commitment to, the Probation Service through teaching, writing and research. Her most recent research on probation officers' workloads, *Workloads: Measurement and Management*, will be published by CEDR/Avebury in autumn 1995.

Colin Pritchard is Professor of Social Work Studies at the University of Southampton. A former Principal Psychiatric Social Worker, he held posts at the Universities of Bath and Leeds before moving to Southampton. His research includes: truancy, international studies of suicide and child abuse. He was lead researcher in the Home Office *Reducing Delinquency* project on effective social work.

Peter Raynor is Reader in Applied Social Studies at University College, Swansea. A former probation officer, he is a leading author in the field of criminal justice policy and probation practice.

Gill Stewart has written extensively in the fields of social work, social policy and the Probation Service. Lecturer at the University of Lancaster, she has recently been closely involved in the monitoring of the social fund and research into the social circumstances of probation clients.

Maurice Vanstone is Lecturer in Applied Social Studies at University College, Swansea and Senior Probation Officer with Mid Glamorgan Probation Service. He has worked in the Probation Service for 25 years and the university for 15 years and has researched and published on a wide range of criminal justice and probation issues.

1 Introduction

Mark Drakeford and Maurice Vanstone

The recent history of the Probation Service has been well documented and discussed (McWilliams, 1987; Raynor *et al.*, 1994). It has been a period of considerable change which has culminated in the most serious threat yet to its value base. The threat is contained within a number of distinct but related sources. Government ministers publicly pronounce the need for a tougher, disciplinary culture while proposing the removal of the training of probation officers from higher education, its separation from social work (Home Office, 1995a); and the replacement of the probation order with a new community sentence designed to strengthen punishment in the community (Home Office, 1995b). Combined with increasingly rigid and prescriptive National Standards (Home Office, 1995c) these proposals feed the delusion that offending can be positively influenced by crude doses of discipline and punishment applied to the 'wicked'. They also conveniently obscure the social context of crime. The central argument of this book is that in its latest period, at least, those in the driving seat of the Service have neglected that context. At the same time there has been, it is important for us to acknowledge, a positive commitment to practise initiatives informed by effectiveness research. However, despite unequivocal messages in the research writings that an individualised focus without a corollary concern with wider social problems is likely to fail (Ross and Fabiano, 1985), the very same research has ironically fostered that narrow focus. We do not intend in this book to denigrate or devalue the efforts of practitioners who are developing empirically informed work with individuals. Instead, we endorse a dual strategy for the Service that involves influencing systems as well as individuals, because like Hudson (1993) we do not see crime as simply 'the outcome of individual's reasoned decision-making' devoid of a structural context.

It is because of the Probation Service's neglect that the attempt to influence systems which form part of that structural context is the main subject of this

1

book. It is an idea which brings forth a number of contradictory responses within the Service itself, one of which is to assert that this idea is simply common sense and common practice which does not require articulation or exploration. Probation officers, it is said, have always been involved in this sort of work and regard it as an integral part of their day-to-day practice. The evidence which we present suggests both that the rhetoric outstrips reality and that, if such activity was once firmly in the mainstream, it is a way of working which has gone rapidly and recently out of fashion.

A more prevalent response is to be found in the idea that probation officers no longer have the scope for working to influence social systems because they have to concentrate upon influencing directly the 'offending behaviour' of their clients. 'Offending behaviour', it may fairly be conceded, began as a useful corrective to that tendency to discuss almost anything with probation clients other than the reason which had brought them to the Service in the first place. As the years of Conservative administration have ground on, however, it has too often been part of the reason for the neglect of the conditions in which crime is created and the devaluation of the social context in which people who offend have to live out their lives. In its most exaggerated form it has at times replaced a proper concern with the human value of probation encounters with a macho insistence on tackling, confronting and acting upon the deviancy of those whom it was otherwise enjoined to advise, assist and befriend.

It seems to us that work which draws individuals to examine their behaviour within a context of social relations, and against a proper concern about the causing of harm – which in effect accords them respect as moral agents – will and should remain a legitimate part of probation activity. However, it must be balanced by an awareness of the limited choices and closed opportunities of probation clients, and a preoccupation with the 'less comfortable and accessible task of addressing structural issues with clients' (Cochrane, 1989: 178).

Our concern is also with the nature of the relationship between probation staff and their clients. A collaborative approach to work which involves strategies designed to effect change in others implies a cooperative relationship. We know that clients value relationships which are based among other things on respect and trust, the capacity to be listened to without being condemned and the provision of relevant help (Bailey and Ward, 1993). Among those whose experience on the receiving end of the criminal justice system is greatest, a single message emerges as the most powerful: the quality sought by long-term prisoners from probation representatives is that of authentic human contact and a quality of contact which produces confidence that client and worker are involved in a process in which both are prepared to make an investment (Williams, 1991). It is implicit in the understanding of this book that without such relationships attempts to help and have an impact on offending will be thwarted.

We, therefore, argue that of all the different – and competing – processes which culminated in the Criminal Justice Act 1991, the replacement of cooperative by coercive relationships threatens to be the most important. Given that crime is predominantly rooted in culturally defined masculinities predicated upon dominance, competition and power, it is ironic that a macho style of management has permeated the Service, with maingrade staff judged by their 'competency' to put into mechanical operation policy decisions and procedural mandates formulated far away from the realities of daily practice. Government prescriptions are clear: probation is now an activity to be carried out upon, rather than with, its recipients: compliance, not cooperation is the keynote of the *National Standards*.

If, at its best, a focus on the offending of individuals can be a creative and innovative attempt to help and initiate change based on choice and collaboration, at its worst 'offending behaviour' becomes a conduit for the kind of ideology described above, and combines a series of ingredients which place a veneer of respectability upon a dubious and most certainly ineffective form of practice. These include a convenient adherence to the idea that individual moral responsibility exists within a vacuum somehow detached from the circumstances in which people might find themselves, and an equally convenient belief that this equality of moral responsibility disappears once an offence has been committed. Within this way of thinking 'offenders' clearly occupy so residual a category of citizenship as to endorse the spirit of moral superiority which suffuses the idea of one human being 'confronting' or 'tackling' the behaviour of another. It is our contention that the routine use of the label 'offender' confirms their place in that category, and accordingly we have endeavoured to limit its use in our contributions. Within the particular context of this book it further licenses a way of regarding the social circumstances of people in trouble as beyond the legitimate scope of state-sponsored intervention. If those who commit offences are responsible for their own plight – as the poor are for their own poverty or the homeless for their lack of shelter – then the upshot is swiftly 'a theory which simultaneously blames the victim and bolsters an unwarranted collective smugness amongst the prosperous' (Jeffs and Smith, 1994: 23). It certainly means that punishment and coercion rather than help and assistance have become their just deserts.

If all this were not sufficiently problematic, the context in which the Probation Service currently operates brings with it a further series of difficulties. The tenets of the 'justice model' reached their high water mark in the 1991 Act which, according to some commentators, was the first Criminal Justice Act ever to be based upon a coherent theoretical view of the sentencing and allied processes. The principle of 'just deserts' was expressed in the White Paper which preceded the Act in this way: 'Punishment in proportion to the seriousness of the crime has long been accepted as one of the many objectives of sentencing. It should be the principal focus for sentencing decisions' (Home Office, 1990). Individuals are personally responsible for their own actions. The task of the criminal justice process is to assess the seriousness of any wrongdoing and to inflict punishment in proportion to that seriousness. As Canton (1993: 7) puts it, the model 'insists on individual responsibility and has no truck with economic, social or psychological explanations of offending. These are relegated to the status of (at best) mitigating factors or (at worst) excuses.' The attraction of the approach to liberals lay in the corollary that no one should be punished more than is warranted by the seriousness of their current offences. The Act's promise strictly to limit the influence of previous convictions, to eliminate deterrence and abandon prevalence as factors in sentencing undoubtedly contributed to the welcome which it received in some practice and academic quarters.

Some commentators (Raynor *et al.*, 1994) while criticising those aspects of the Act have argued that the according of a central role to the pre-sentence report presented a positive opportunity to the Probation Service. Subsequent changes brought about by legislation and government directives have diminished that opportunity; however, when Courts do consider pre-sentence reports the potential for positive influence remains. Yet, as a basis for social work intervention in the criminal justice system the Act, and its version of just deserts, was badly flawed from the outset. In particular, the deliberate devaluation of personal and social circumstances and their impact upon individual actions flies in the face of accumulated knowledge and understanding which accelerated rather than diminished during the Thatcher years. Moreover, as John Pitts has pointed out, the social circumstances of adult defendants are likely to be both more complex and differently regarded by sentencers – 'more culpable, intractable and deserving of punishment' (Pitts, 1992: 140) – than in the practice with juveniles upon the success of which the changes had been based. Older defendants have children of their own; they will almost certainly be unemployed and likely to live in unsatisfactory accommodation. The degree of moral autonomy and responsibility which may properly be attributed to them will be complicated, at least, by the extent to which they are subject to mental illness or acting under the influence of drugs and alcohol.

The combination of 'macho-correctionalism' and 'radical managerialism' (Pitts, 1992) produces a practice which neglects the diversity and complexity of real life in favour of the simple rigidities of standard procedures. In doing so it achieves the worst of a series of different worlds. First, it withdraws from engagement in the concerns which are important to the individuals on the receiving end of supervision and reduces very significantly the worth of work which might be undertaken. Second, in its willingness to reduce the face-to-face encounters of fruitful social work to a series of formulaic confrontations it also prepares the ground for those political forces anxious to de-professionalise the public services and replace thoughtful and critical practitioners with a new, poorly paid, lightly skilled and automatically obedient workforce. Third, it fails to deliver a product which is of lasting value to the Courts. Sentencers look to the Probation Service to provide help and assistance to those individuals whom it commits to its charge. While evidence of thorough and consistent exercise of this remit is important, efficiency and effectiveness cannot be established through procedures which, bureaucratically rather than practice focused, appear designed to demonstrate the inevitable and inherent impossibility of making progress.

Even if the 1991 Act were to be regarded as an acceptable basis for practice, however, the decisions made in the 24 months which followed its enactment in October 1992 dismantled its provisions, one by one. The ink was barely dry upon a statue which the Home Secretary of the time, David Waddington, had lauded as 'going with the grain of history, not against it' when it came under an orchestrated attack in which Government ministers enthusiastically joined. The principle of punishment limited to the seriousness of any offence had already been qualified in the Act in respect of sexual or other violent offences for which additional punishment, beyond that deserved by the seriousness of any crime committed, could be imposed if considered necessary for the protection of the public. The Court of Appeal now set about reassembling the previous status quo in other respects. The Cunningham judgement of 1993 found that, despite the removal of deterrence – the notion that defendants should be additionally punished to prevent them from doing things they had not yet done – the Act's words 'commensurate with the seriousness of the offence' really meant commensurate with future deterrence as well. The same judgment also dispensed with the Act's limitations upon prevalence – the notion that one person could be punished more harshly than their conduct deserved because other people might be committing other offences of their own – on the basis that the actions of these other people made the offence before the Court more serious than would otherwise be the case.

Of the four limitations identified by Canton only one remained: the ambiguities of Section 29 of the Act and its effect upon the extent to which defendants could be punished again for offences already punished previously by the Courts. When the Court of Appeal – grudgingly – confirmed the meaning of the original Act, the Government came to the rescue by repealing the section altogether. The last remnant of a justice approach had been removed.

It is against this background that the Probation Service needs so badly to reinvest itself in ways of working which are rooted in its own distinctive tradition and contribution to the workings of a criminal justice system which has become the most vengeful and voracious in the whole of Western Europe. Defensiveness and a covert, shame-faced adherence to basic principles will not do. Instead we need to assert the case for active intervention by probation officers in the social worlds which their clients inhabit. Effective impact upon offending depends upon addressing those elements within an individual's life and circumstances in which that offending is rooted. Despite the threatening environment, we believe that the history and traditions of the Service, its self-critical nature and its personnel, leave it still in shape to pick up that challenge. However, it can only do so if it invests the same amount of energy invested in the pursuit of empirically informed practice with individuals, into broader strategies aimed at contributing to the improvement in the lives of those people to whom it provides a service. We agree with Broad and Denny (1992) about the need for a shift in power towards those people, and the range of ideas in the Charter which they have set out could be a contribution to that shift. We know, however, that the gloss of charters is soon dulled by a lack of accompanying action; so a real shift in power will only come about when Probation Service policies and strategies focus on the wider context of offending.

This book is an attempt to show why and how this should and can be done (and in some areas, is being done). We have deliberately concentrated on five key areas, the criminal justice system itself and those basic props of money, work, housing and health which allow the fortunate to keep their lives on an even keel. All contributors share a central theme: that probation officers seeking to do some good in their clients' lives and to assist them to trouble-free behaviour must, of necessity, direct their attention to those social systems which support such possibilities. The ways in which social systems might best be influenced are more a matter of debate and difference. This book is intended to be a contribution to that necessary debate. The engagement of Probation Services and workers with the wider social contexts of their clients' lives has been so in retreat that there are no reliable taken-for-granted wisdoms to support a reinvestment in these processes now. Indeed, the world has changed so significantly in the past 15 years that a simple return to former ways of working would, in any case, be ill-attuned to present conditions.

The book begins with Peter Raynor's chapter which considers the influence of the Probation Service within the criminal justice system itself. Raynor suggests a number of important themes which also resonate in other contributions. He points out that the rhetoric of Service influence upon the criminal justice process is not matched by performance – or, indeed, by a necessary willingness to act in a way which promotes influence. It is a theme which pervades this book. One of the reasons for assembling this text has been to call into question the taken-for-granted idea that probation work is about intervening in systems for the benefit of its clients. Raynor shows that even closest to home the Probation Service has been over-preoccupied with the development of its own programmes and procedures to the neglect of understanding the ways in which these activities might influence other parts of the criminal justice system.

In a second theme this chapter also highlights the damage which has been done to the Service's capacity for effective influence by its increasing reliance upon Home Office direction. The sudden and incoherent reversals which have marked Home Office policy-making during the mid-1990s have left the Service cruelly exposed – alternately seduced and bullied to a reluctant altar, only to be abandoned before the reception has even been cleared away.

Raynor also sets out a series of issues to which successful attempts at influencing systems need to attend. First, he shows how policy itself in this area is not enough. It is the practical implementation of policy by individual workers that has the greatest impact and that implementation is most frequently in the hands of workers at team and local level. Second, he suggests that interagency work has to command a greater priority if systems are to be influenced most effectively, and points to the traditional reluctance of the Probation Service to work in a genuinely cooperative and power-sharing way with others. Third, he emphasises the importance of the community context for probation activities. If the outcomes of the criminal justice system for individuals are to be improved, then the resources of local communities will have to be more effectively mobilised, and attitudes within the community towards people who offend will have to be understood and taken into account. Indeed, in his fourth element in systems intervention Raynor lays particular emphasis upon the importance of attitude change, independent of legislative or organisational amendments, in altering outcomes. It is an idea which pervades the remaining chapters of the book because attitudes towards probation clients by providers of other social systems are often the first and most powerful stumbling block in obtaining access to the services which they control. The practical operation of this influence is readily identified by probation clients themselves. In their study of probation clients as victims of crime, for example, Peelo *et al.* (1992) found that it was the denial of victim status – because they themselves had been offenders – which was experienced as one of the harshest consequences of having a crime committed against themselves. Police officers would not take reports of such crimes seriously, housing officers reacted without sympathy to incidents of theft or damage and social security officers responded to loss or non-arrival of giros as a prima facie cause for suspicion, because the victim had themselves been in trouble.

Attitudes and the policies which produce and sustain them are at the heart of Chapter 3 by Jon Arnold and Bill Jordan. In their account of poverty and its impact upon the work of probation officers they proceed from the basis that the state income maintenance systems in Britain have become so designed to punish and deter poor people that direct engagement with these agencies by probation staff is more likely to produce adverse than worthwhile consequences for clients. While some of their conclusions are contested in the following editorial Commentary section, we are in full agreement with their emphasis upon the need for probation officers to invest themselves in the more local, informal systems which impoverished communities themselves develop in order to combat the effects of malign neglect.

Iain Crow (Chapter 4) provides a salutary reminder that relating unemployment to crime is a complex matter which can only be examined alongside their mutual relationship with matters such as poverty, social deprivation, drug misuse and changes in law enforcement and policy. In a detailed analysis he also provides an explanation of the different ways of looking at the relationship, combined with a perceptive critique of their deficiencies. This chapter includes a summary of the main features of the principal research studies on the subject, which in itself provides a useful framework for Probation Service activity. While he concludes that the high incidence of unemployment among probation clients is not in itself evidence of a link, he elucidates a persuasive argument for the Service engaging with this issue.

Gill Stewart, in her chapter on housing, draws on an astonishing wealth of information gained through direct investigation of the contemporary social circumstances of Probation Service users. Her conclusion is one of the more optimistic of this book's contributors. The evidence for Probation Service investment in strategic intervention in accommodation issues is relatively plentiful. Yet dangers are also clearly apparent. The national fate of public housing has been particularly bleak in the past 15 years and Probation Service achievements are in many ways akin to rolling a stone up an ever-steepening hill.

In Chapter 6 Joan Orme and Colin Pritchard set out clear evidence that a significant proportion of probation caseloads is made up by individuals with mental and drug related problems. They present the argument for the Probation Service to develop strategies based on partnership arrangements against the background of the problems caused to practitioners by the emergence of hospital trusts and GP fundholders. The main argument of this chapter is that a considerable proportion of probation activity in this area will of necessity be undertaken by individual workers who will have to negotiate and collaborate with a range of services involved in the provision of treatment. It concludes by explaining ways in which the Service can have impact on health related problems.

At the end of each chapter we provide a Commentary in which we attempt to respond to the implications for practice as set out by each of the authors. In doing so we draw on a number of examples of good policy and practice initiatives. We appreciate the fact that we have inevitably left out as many equally laudable initiatives. For that we apologise but hope that the probation staff involved in those schemes will draw some comfort from the fact that the general direction of their efforts is given some deserved attention. Finally, readers will find that there is a great deal of cross-referencing to be carried out between the different issues tackled in the book. The basic props of a stable life interact with one another in clear and powerful ways and difficulties in one area quickly lead to knock-on effects in others. We confidently leave readers to make these connections, and in doing so, to draw on the evidence of their own experience.

2 The criminal justice system

Peter Raynor

At first sight it may seem strange or perverse to raise this subject at all. Surely the Probation Service is obviously and self-evidently a constructive influence on the criminal justice system? What other reason could there be for having a Probation Service? Few bodies of professional workers can have re-stated their commitment to social work values with such frequency and determination as probation officers have done, both through their trade union and professional association – National Association of Probation Officers (NAPO) and through their managers' organisation – Association of Chief Officers of Probation (ACOP). If the strength of one's impact on a system depends on the strength of one's assertion that it exists, probation would be unrivalled as the leading influence in criminal justice. The reality is not so straightforward. The purpose of this chapter is to suggest that the influence of Probation Services on both policy and on individual decisions in criminal justice is often not as great nor as positive as it could be. It further suggests that the best results are unlikely to be achieved unless Probation Services combine clarity and honesty about their own distinctive messages and contributions with a willingness to work with other agencies and with the community in implementing change.

First, however, two cautionary notes are in order, both on the theme of not overestimating one's own influence. My former colleague June Lait, who became famous for her polemics against social work (e.g. Brewer and Lait, 1980), was fond of saying that if social workers really could change people, why do they concentrate on the poor and powerless who have few options and little influence, when changing the wealthy and powerful could have so much more effect? Such a question, although no doubt intended to irritate, actually draws our attention to some of the realities of power in criminal justice: a decision made in a few moments by a powerful body such as a Court can sometimes have more influence on the course of an offender's life than many months of effort in a situation where there are few options and

11

little opportunity for change. Influence applied at the point of decision, if successful, may be much more effective than greater inputs at other times. Persuading a Court to make a probation order instead of a custodial sentence may be a far more effective use of time than months of after-care designed to counteract the ill effects of avoidable imprisonment. The difficulty is that the more powerful may be more difficult to influence: they will have more resources and social and ideological supports of their own, and will be less dependent on the social worker's favourable attitude. To exercise influence in these circumstances depends (despite grandiose talk of 'educating the magistrates') on persuasiveness rather than authority, and some examples of how such opportunities are used in practice will be described later in the paper.

The second cautionary note concerns the idea of a system. Our criminal justice 'system' is not a system in the sense of a planned or coherent whole representing a unified approach to problems and subject to rational strategies of overall control. It is not systematic and in many ways not rational. Control over it is fragmented, exercised by different power blocs with their own interests which pull in different directions. At the core of the system lies the fiscal paradox that the executive does not control the actions of the judiciary but must nevertheless pay for them. One Criminal Justice Act after another seeks to impose some unity of purpose and predictability of operation, seldom with more than limited or temporary success. It is notoriously difficult to predict the system's outcomes, trends or costs, and such predictions as are published are often revised within months. Inconsistency, unintended consequences and public and professional dissatisfaction are part of the daily experience of working in the system. Within such an environment, influence may be difficult to exercise and its results hard to predict.

However, it is correct to regard our society's criminal justice activities as a system in the explanatory sense that what is done in one part of it is likely to affect what happens in another, often in surprising ways. The mechanical analogy is not an orderly and predictable structure of rigid links and levers, but a more chaotic or organic assemblage in which diverse subassemblies are connected by a Heath Robinson array of wires, strings and elastic bands. Some influences are one-way (strings will pull but not push); others are partial (elastic bands transmit some motion and absorb the rest as strain). Intervention in such complexity can be a delicate and provisional business, with outcomes which are hard to predict and which remain unknown unless they are observed and measured.

Systems as targets and opportunities

The idea that social work practice consists largely of attempts to influence systems is not new, and was the basis of an influential American attempt to restate social work's claims as a unified profession. The 'unitary method' of Pincus and Minahan (1973), in particular, described almost any target of intervention as a 'system', and they were accused of a conservative preoccupation with maintaining the functioning of systems (Leonard, 1975). This was unfair: in fact they distinguish clearly between 'target systems' and beneficiaries (or 'client systems'). The purpose of intervention can be to influence the former in the interests of the latter. This was a constructive and radical proposal in a social work context where 'clients' were too often the sole recipients of attention which could have been directed to influencing others on their behalf, and where a major social work textbook could base itself on an explicitly consensual idea of 'maintenance' as the primary and distinctive goal of social work (Davies, 1981). 'Maintenance' in criminal justice could mean simply going along with the system's drift, having no professional objectives beyond fitting in. The American 'systems theories' of social work encouraged some exploration of alternatives, and specific alternative approaches in criminal justice were also encouraged by the radical criminologies of the 1960s. These tended to advocate decriminalisation, diversion and decarceration as strategies for reform, and when seen from this perspective the criminal justice system presents itself as a loose articulation of decision-making points at which influence could potentially be exercised.

The extent of indeterminacy and discretion in the system is neatly illustrated by the Home Office's own statistical material. Only half of the estimated total of offences is reported: victims may believe nothing can be done, or that the offence is too trivial, or that they will themselves be treated unsympathetically by police. Only three-fifths of reported offences are recorded as offences: police discretion to 'no crime' an offence is widely used, for example to avoid recording offences which are unlikely ever to be cleared up and will therefore make clear-up rates look worse. Even so, less than a quarter of those recorded are cleared up, and only 2 per cent, or one in fifty of the original offences committed, result in a conviction. The vast majority of these result in non-custodial sentences. Conviction and punishment by a criminal court is actually one of the least common ways of dealing with crime, and what is described by the Home Office as 'attrition' also points to the number and range of diversion opportunities within the system. Most obviously, discretion operates at the point of entry to the system and determines whether a problem is to become an issue for the formal criminal justice system or not; it operates at the point of decision whether or not to prosecute and it operates after prosecution, both in relation to guilt and innocence and in relation to sentence. From the point of view of agencies or professionals concerned to reduce reliance on official coercion as a response to social problems, these discretion points represent the most obvious opportunities for diversionary practice.

Systems for juveniles but not adults?

The language of diversion first gained widespread currency in the Probation Service following the Wootton report on non-custodial and semi-custodial penalties (Advisory Council on the Penal System, 1970) which explicitly identified itself with a policy of reducing the use of expensive and ineffective custodial sentences for minor offenders. The innovations which followed in the Criminal Justice Act 1972 included some with a specifically diversionary rationale: most obviously, the main aim of community service was to provide constructive non-custodial punishment, and the Day Training Centres were also aimed at a clientele which would otherwise be in prison. Home Office research on Community Service was almost exclusively concerned with the extent to which it displaced custody. In the 'nothing works' era, when research on the effectiveness of sentencing held out little hope of rehabilitative impact (Martinson, 1974; Brody, 1976), reducing custodial sentencing seemed a valuable and achievable goal in its own right: it also might save money and at least seemed unlikely to do harm. However, much of the Probation Service seemed curiously half-hearted in pursuit of this goal. Practitioners were still committed to a style of work which presupposed at least the possibility of rehabilitative effectiveness, and some of them resented developments like Community Service because they seemed to marginalise rehabilitative goals and to open the way to non-professional staffing. Opposition to such developments thus reflected a happy coincidence of principle and self-interest. Throughout the 1970s and much of the 1980s it remained unusual for any Probation Service to evaluate its practice by measures relevant to diversionary aims, such as comparisons between local and national sentencing trends: indeed empirical evaluation of any kind was a rarity.

In juvenile justice the concept of system intervention was more readily embraced following pioneering studies by the Lancaster group (Thorpe *et al.*, 1980). Their studies of local authority practice showed a tendency for over-intervention to fail and to push young people towards custodial sentences: the diversionary intentions of the 1969 Children and Young Persons Act were resulting in an alarming increase in juvenile incarceration because practice was not sufficiently informed by understanding of the juvenile justice system and by strategies to influence its operation. What eventually emerged to counteract this was a diversionary practice based on careful use of information about local juvenile justice systems and about the impact of social work activities on them. Juvenile justice practice during the 1980s provided the first examples of the systematic use of local sentencing information and of evaluative information about the outcomes of social inquiry reports. In due course this 'systems approach' expanded to include interagency work to promote cautioning, to avoid custodial remands, and to develop and promote new community alternatives such as mediation. Overall, the approach could claim some spectacular successes, and particularly the number of young people receiving custodial sentences declined steadily.

Many probation officers were aware of, and indeed were involved in these developments, but somehow the equivalent approaches in the adult criminal justice system never fully took off. Hindsight suggests a number of reasons for this. Adult offenders often had longer offending histories and seemed less likely to 'grow out' of crime, so arguments based on minimum intervention were less persuasive; also probation officers traditionally prided themselves on a greater degree of professional autonomy than local authority workers, and ideas like a corporate policy on recommendations in social inquiry reports often encountered resistance within the culture of the service. Probation Services were slow to adopt the kind of information systems and information-led policy and practice models which could support an empirical approach to influencing systems. Having managed without such information for decades, and not being accustomed to having much to learn from the practice of Social Services Departments, perhaps some Probation Services were slow to see the need. For whatever reasons, the dramatic results produced by quite small teams of juvenile justice specialists in some (by no means all) local authorities seemed likely to elude many Probation Services. When the Criminal Justice Act 1982 attempted to strengthen statutory safeguards against custodial sentencing and to encourage the development of high-tariff probation orders incorporating special programmes of activity for offenders who might otherwise be in prison, some officers embraced the new opportunities but many were sceptical. They argued that they were being 'set up to fail' since they could not really expect to influence the Courts' excessive use of custody.

Some similar feelings were aroused by the publication in 1984 of the first comprehensive Home Office statement about the Probation Service's functions and purposes, the 'Statement of National Objectives and Priorities' (Home Office, 1994b). Without actually saying so, the Statement was clearly rooted in a system management perspective and saw the Service as the instrument which could be used to persuade sentencers to prefer supervision in the community to custodial sentences. Performance indicators were developed to measure Service performance against the Statement, and the nature of some key indicators clearly reveals their diversionary intent: for example, indicators included the proportion of probationers who were first offenders (intended to decrease) and the proportion who had previously been to prison (intended to increase). Although some probation managers have since complained that this approach holds Probation Services accountable for sentencing outcomes which are not under their control, the influence of a 'systems' perspective on the Statement was clear.

What was less clear was exactly how these results were to be achieved: in the juvenile system, much of the development of methods and practice had proceeded in partnerships of statutory and voluntary agencies funded and monitored by the DHSS and the Welsh Office for that specific purpose, and it is arguable that without this earmarked funding local authorities would not have made comparable progress on their own. In the adult system, there was less reliance on earmarked funding of development projects apart from a handful of intensive supervision schemes, and Probation Services were left to develop their own practice. While this produced some outstandingly useful innovations such as the widespread adoption of 'risk of custody' scales to guide report writers, it seldom produced an integrated strategy to influence local decisions which was fully reflected in probation officers' practice. Although there was widespread evidence of upward movement in the 'tariff' level of probation orders, it was usually much harder to see whether this was affecting local sentencing patterns. When the Green Paper *Punishment, Custody and Community* (Home Office, 1988a) made explicit links between the successes of juvenile justice policy and the Government's future aims for the Probation Service, discussion was focused far more on the paper's punitive rhetoric than on its specific proposals for future criminal justice strategy.

Further confusion was sown when the 1991 Act incorporated sentencing requirements clearly designed to reduce the use of imprisonment, as prefigured in a White Paper which described prison as 'an expensive way of making bad people worse' (Home Office, 1990a), but at the same time discouraged the language of 'alternatives to custody' and made the probation order a sentence in its own right. Previous convictions (the main basis of 'risk of custody' scales) temporarily disappeared as a central influence in sentencing, to be replaced by a concept of 'seriousness' which was morally fitting but hard to quantify. Eventually, having made the most serious and comprehensive attempt yet to address its responsibility for system management and for developing an integrated criminal justice policy, the Government panicked at the possibility that these reforms might appear insufficiently punitive, and decided to reverse many of them even before evidence of their impact was available. One would have to search deep in the history of criminal justice to find a shabbier betrayal of all principles of sound policy-making; fortunately there is little sign that it has yielded the short-term political gains for which the Government presumably hoped. However, the effects on Probation Services, and on other services within criminal justice, have been uniformly unsettling and confusing: the more they have relied on the Home Office to determine the direction of policy, the more difficult it has become to know what to do when more and more policy reversals emerge from the Criminal Justice Act 1993 and the Criminal Justice and Public Order Act 1994. The remainder of this chapter makes a few suggestions about how Probation

Services might think about and develop their role in the system without being quite so dependent on the Home Office to show them the way ahead.

The need for much strategic thinking within and about probation has been underlined yet again by the publication of a new Green Paper on 'strengthening punishment in the community' (Home Office, 1995b) and by new proposals on the training of probation officers (Dews and Watts, 1995; Home Office, 1995a). These linked initiatives appear to form part of a conscious attempt by the right wing of the Conservative Party to change the culture of the Probation Service in a direction more consistent with the Government's latest penal policy. Under these proposals, the probation order itself will disappear subsumed by a new 'Integrated Community Sentence', which will no longer require the offender's consent; and the training of probation officers will no longer be part of social work training, and will take place outside universities in a much reduced in-service form. Clearly both social work values and university education are seen as potentially contaminating for the Probation Service of the future (Williams, 1994). Such developments challenge the Probation Service of the present to develop and articulate its identity, before this is done for it by others.

Monitoring and outcomes: the example of reports

Historically, Probation Services have often been better at devising and announcing policies than at monitoring and evaluating practice to see how far it reflects intended policy. As I indicated above, the development of monitoring was essential in the evolution of 'systems' approaches; the dangers of developing policy without adequate monitoring are obvious, particularly in criminal justice systems so prone to deliver unintended consequences. To take just one of the identified points of influence in the system, some recent research on reports to sentencers provides useful examples both of unintended consequences and of the beneficial effects of getting things right.

Before the 1991 Act was implemented, many defendants appearing in Crown Courts were sentenced without social inquiry reports, and one Probation Service took advantage of this to undertake a systematic study of what happened to similar offenders when they were sentenced with or without the benefit of a report (Raynor, 1991). Like other studies, this showed that the availability of reports was associated with a higher use of what later came to be known as 'community sentences', namely probation and community service, but for one group in particular there was also a paradoxical result: older adults (21 and over) who had a 'medium' risk of custody were twice as likely to receive an immediate custodial sentence if they were sentenced with the aid of a report (37 per cent of this group were sentenced to immediate custody, compared with 18 per cent of similar offenders sentenced without a report). The most common non-custodial sentences for those sentenced without reports were fines and suspended sentences, but these options hardly figured among probation officers' recommendations: instead they offered probation or community service orders, and when sentencers rejected these the result tended to be a custodial sentence. The report of the research concludes that there is scope for considering the pattern of recommendations, but also points out that such studies are well within the scope of most Probation Services to undertake: there is no need for unexpected or unintended outcomes to remain unknown, but in the absence of monitoring they will do so. We cannot influence systems if we do not even know the immediate consequences of our own inputs.

The second example goes some way towards contradicting the widespread belief that to expect the Probation Service to have an impact on systems is to expect the impossible, holding it accountable for decisions beyond its control and 'setting it up to fail'. Certainly this kind of strategy relies on influence rather than on power to control, and on influence by persuasion rather than by simple authority; this should appeal to probation officers who resist definition of their task as control. However, recent research shows that influence by persuasion can have real effects, provided that the quality of service is high. The evidence comes from a study of the quality and impact of a large sample of pre-sentence reports presented in the Crown Courts which showed not only that the quality of report writing is remarkably variable (Gelsthorpe and Raynor, 1993) but that the better-quality reports are more likely to result in community sentences, and less likely to result in custodial sentences (Gelsthorpe and Raynor, 1995). Past attempts to study the effectiveness of reports may have found it difficult to do so partly because they were not able to distinguish between good and bad reports; the recent evidence, however, suggests that the better reports are more likely to be persuasive, and that a strategy of influencing the system through report writing needs to include systematic quality controls.

The general point is that it is insufficient to have a policy: we also need procedures to deliver practice that accords with the policy, and methods of monitoring both the practice and its outcomes. Similar points could be made about other interventions in the system: for example, avoidable incarceration occurs through fine default and through refusal of bail as well as through sentencing, and although there have been initiatives to address these, they are piecemeal and not consistently evaluated. The recent national inspection of bail information schemes identifies a need for 'better management and monitoring' (Home Office, 1993a).

Importantly, the same report identifies a need for more interagency collaboration. This is another feature of successful system management strategies in juvenile justice: all relevant parties meet and communicate and, where possible, plan together. Interagency liaison was also a feature of the Woolf report's recommendations (Woolf, 1991), out of which grew a system of Area Criminal Justice Committees, but these operate largely at senior management level when the lessons of most experience and research suggest that liaison at practitioner and middle manager level is more fruitful. With a few notable exceptions (such as Hampshire's interagency sentencing initiative – Hampshire Probation Service, 1992), Probation Services do not have an outstanding record in interagency or community work (Henderson, 1987), and this is a disadvantage in working with others to influence systems. In general, most Probation Services have in the past been better at using their own resources to develop new ways of supervising offenders than at working with others to develop influence in systems. This is not simply an issue for managers, as the Statement of National Objectives and Priorities mistakenly implied, but for all practitioners, working with an awareness of common policy and direction.

Current problems and the dynamics of system change

One reason for underlining the importance of working with others is that what little knowledge we have about the dynamics of system change suggests that it is not brought about simply by the right technical inputs, or by selling the right options to decision-makers. Influencing the way other actors in the system think is probably more important than trying to manipulate them towards particular outcomes. For example, researchers who have studied the quite rapid reduction in custodial sentencing in (West) Germany during the early 1980s have pointed not to specific practice or legal innovations but to a general change of view among a wide range of criminal justice professionals, leading to an emerging consensus that prison was not usually constructive. Importantly, this change involved lawyers and politicians as well as social workers, sentencers and many police. Community alternatives to prison were important in contributing to a climate of opinion, but accounted numerically for only a small part of the substantial displacement from custody (Feest, 1988).

Ominously, there is evidence that similar processes can also work in the opposite direction. American criminologists suggest that the huge increase in imprisonment in California is the cumulative result of quite small shifts in opinion and practice, and particularly of hard-line rhetoric by politicians, rather than of any particular change in legislation (Zimring and Hawkins, 1994). Our own Government's sentencing statistics show how the very substantial reduction in imprisonment following implementation of the 1991

Act in October 1992 began to reverse itself quite early in 1993 well before any changes in legislation were actually made (Home Office, 1994a). This seems again to demonstrate the power of political statements which signal a more punitive policy.

The general lesson seems to be that changes in criminal justice systems need to be prefigured, exemplified and supported. In other words, the ideas behind them need to be articulated, discussed with others and openly debated, and some practical initiatives based on those ideas need to be developed and evaluated, to demonstrate their feasibility. The strategy is about winning support for ideas, arguments and values as much as for specific policies or programmes, and the aim is a climate of informed opinion favourable to the right kind of developments. For a while, during the development and implementation of the 1991 Act, it seemed we were close to a reformist consensus in England and Wales, with the Probation Service centrally involved. The current reversal of this consensus is a bitter disappointment, but it contains its own contradictions and instabilities and seems likely to be temporary. In this context Probation Services need to maintain the arguments of expediency, economy and effectiveness that pointed to community sentencing as the best option in the past, but arguably they should go further and engage also in the moral and political arguments. In common with Nellis (1995) I would suggest a need for Probation Services to explore, develop and articulate their own distinctive vision of criminal justice based on such values as inclusion, reconciliation, restorative justice and crime reduction.

In an address to a NAPO professional conference ten years ago I argued that the only way to break the vicious circle by which community anger at increasing crime leads to more punitive and ineffective policies is to adopt a realistic approach to communicating about crime, and to show how more constructive policies will meet the real and justifiable concerns of victims and potential victims. Some of the audience told me it was very right-wing to mention victims. Sadly, politicians have shown themselves prepared to exploit and manipulate the anger of victims and of communities suffering from inadequate and ineffective criminal justice services. These voices are unlikely to go quiet again: the people they represent are unlikely to resume a respectful and deferential posture of leaving everything to the experts. Probation Services need to establish a dialogue with the communities they serve and to listen to them, if the ideas they seek to embody in criminal justice are going to command understanding and support. At the very least, the task of communicating publicly about crime should not be left to politicians, since they cannot be relied upon to perform it responsibly.

Influencing systems, then, is necessary, possible and sometimes achievable. It requires clarity of purpose, strategy and implementation; it requires humility and honesty in measuring what actually results; it requires open communication with others and a willingness to listen; and now more than ever, it requires realism about the extent and impact of crime.

Editors' commentary

This Commentary section sets out to illustrate some of the ways in which the Probation Service is involved in systems-focused work within criminal justice itself. These are initiatives which have, as their main aim, the creation of change within that system, rather than in the individuals over whom supervision is exercised on behalf of the Courts. For, as Peter Raynor makes clear, the effort to influence the criminal justice processes which most fundamentally affect those individuals is a basic and fruitful investment in influencing the course of their own future behaviour.

The most thorough-going attempts to affect individual offending patterns through systems intervention are to be found in the field of youth justice. Ironically – but usefully – after a period in which the Probation Service negotiated hard to remove itself from involvement in the Juvenile Court, the Criminal Justice Act 1991 creation of the Youth Court has seen it move back into this arena. In doing so it has benefited directly from the experience of social worker colleagues already familiar with systems management approaches. The practical arrangements for social work services in the Youth Court were the subject of some early controversy. The resulting pattern of service delivery has been reported upon by both Social Services and Probation Inspectorates (Department of Health, 1994; Home Office, 1994b). Both reports comment upon the success of pre-court diversion and cautioning schemes in keeping non-serious young offenders from the formal system. Both also note the continuing operation of satisfactory arrangements for contact between practitioners and sentencers. Credibility with other key agencies and service users was the product of considerable investment in this area of work, usually by Social Services Departments. Variation in local arrangement of services was considerable and complex but often legitimate in responding to particular local needs and circumstances.

A good example of some of these themes is to be found in the South Glamorgan arrangements for Youth Court provision. Following the 1991 Act a combined team of probation and social services staff have access to the most comprehensive pre-trial, bail and remand services in Wales (Welsh Office, 1993). The preparation of pre-sentence reports (PSRs) is overseen by a weekly Community Sentencing Panel involving both agencies and Barnardos, the main local voluntary sector partner in the provision of community options. The panel operates an effective gatekeeping arrangement, scrutinising reports and proposals in order to ensure that basic principles of maximum diversion, minimum appropriate intervention and systems management apply in all PSRs to be presented to the Court.

The panel and report writers benefit from the work of the Youth Court Bureau, a joint arrangement with the South Wales Police which has halved the length of time between arrest for an offence and that offence being dealt with by the Courts. Peter Raynor suggests that effort invested in systems approaches of this sort has a direct benefit for Service strategies aimed at influencing the offending of its clients. The South Glamorgan Bureau success in shortening the length of time between arrest and Court decision has produced a 69 per cent reduction in the number of offences committed by young people awaiting sentence (South Glamorgan, 1994). Given that Courts are now obliged to regard offences committed on bail as an aggravating factor in determining sentence the systems outcome has a clear and additional impact in this regard.

While Probation Services now take part more fully in such joint arrangements in Youth Justice there is also growing evidence of wider interest in establishing and validating the role which the Service might play in pre-trial work within the adult courts. Activity in this context is already widespread but characterised by isolated initiatives, sustained by local enthusiasms. Work also proceeds in piecemeal fashion, with links only prefiguratively drawn between the different initiatives. Two broad groups may however be discerned. The first aims to divert either individuals or groups of individuals from criminal prosecution altogether. These initiatives include public interest case assessment and adult cautioning schemes. The second aims to influence the progress of individuals through the process from arrest to sentence in a way which has an impact upon the different decisions made about those individuals at these different stages. These schemes include services for mentally disordered offenders discussed elsewhere in this book and bail information and bail support schemes. In this Commentary we aim to look briefly at one example from each of these groups.

Of those initiatives which aim to remove people altogether from prosecution, Public Interest Case Assessment (PICA) schemes have been the subject of the most thorough monitoring and evaluation. The Vera Institute (Stone, 1989), the Home Office Research Unit (Brown and Crisp, 1992) and individual schemes have all reported on activity in this area. The longest standing programme has been that run by the Inner London Probation Service. In its current guise it provides information to the Crown Prosecution Service (CPS) in order to allow that Service to decide on whether or not prosecution might be discontinued in the public interest. The scheme works with people charged with relatively non-serious offences – theft (but not burglary), criminal damage, charges arising from Sections 4 and 5 of the Public Order Act 1986 and charges of drunk and disorderly behaviour. No offences of violence come within the scheme. Working to criteria set out within the CPS Code Of

Practice, probation officers offer the chance of interview to individuals following a first Court appearance. Attendance at interview is entirely voluntary. If the information forthcoming suggests that the offence concerned is so trivial as likely to end in a nominal penalty, or if the individual concerned would be unduly affected by prosecution because of youth, old age or infirmity or if prosecution might have an adverse effect on the individual on grounds of mental illness or stress then that prosecution can be discontinued as not in the public interest.

Information passed to the CPS is made available to the individual concerned and their solicitor. It is not presented in Court. It does, however, act as some counterweight to the police evidence upon which the CPS must otherwise rely and allows for some resistance to both 'passive acquiescence' and 'prosecutorial momentum' (Brown and Crisp, 1992) in which the decision to prosecute, once taken, proves very difficult to reverse.

In the three years of the scheme 1990–3, between a quarter and one-third of cases reported upon resulted in discontinuation of prosecution. Of those some 40 per cent have been because of information relevant to the mental health/stress criteria, a finding consistent with the practice examples cited in the Commentary section at the end of Chapter 6. The involvement of Probation Service workers has been crucial in this regard. The verification of information through contact with other social welfare and health professionals, together with mobilisation of necessary help to diminish the likelihood of further offending is a task which, within the criminal justice system, probation officers are uniquely qualified to undertake. As well as these clear benefits to individuals, the scheme is also plainly effective in a systemic sense. It reduces the number of trivial and unnecessary cases within an overloaded court system, it prevents the far more labour-intensive preparation of pre-sentence reports by the Probation Service at a later stage and, by keeping vulnerable and impressionable people out of the system altogether contributes significantly to the chances of their avoiding further offences.

At the time of writing PICA schemes appear to have entered that limbo which the current regime at the Home Office reserves for worthwhile and useful schemes. As the ACOP Pre-trial Working Group, looking to develop interagency services, puts it 'there is little prospect of the Home Office giving any active support' (ACOP, 1994. 2). The cash-limiting of individual Service budgets and the devolution of financial management within Probation Services also means that activity outside core statutory responsibilities comes under ever-greater scrutiny and pressure. The argument of this Commentary is that an ever-narrowing definition of Probation Service functions and consequent service provision is doubly damaging both in the wider sense and in the particular focus of tackling offending. PICA schemes and the development of adult cautioning, by contrast, provide a dual set of benefits:

they contribute to general improvements within the criminal justice system and they add specifically to the longer term goals of the Probation Service.

The second example from this group of pre-trial initiatives is drawn from those schemes which do not seek to divert individuals from prosecution altogether but which attempt instead to influence decisions made at pre-sentence points within the process. Bail information and bail support services aim to influence decisions which Courts might make, either by providing information which allows the Crown Prosecution Service not to oppose bail or to allow the Courts to avoid a remand into custody. These decisions are of great importance in at least three different ways.

First, there is the immediate impact upon individuals and their ability to maintain vital aspects of their lives during the pre-sentence period. The interconnectedness of the main topics covered in this book is nowhere more apparent than in the direct effect which decisions to bail or remand in custody have upon the accommodation, employment and health of the individuals concerned.

Second, the decision as to bail has an immediate impact upon the number of people held in custody. As the Commentary on the housing chapter of this book suggests, the failure of the Home Office to provide the promised number of beds in bail hostels was certainly among the factors contributing to the 30 per cent rise in the remand population which took place during the 12 months to April 1994. By allowing individuals who would otherwise be in custody to remain outside prison yet more overcrowding in those parts of the system where unconvicted people are held – that is to say, where the most pressurised and inhumane conditions prevail – are avoided. As 68 per cent of defendants held in custody never return to prison after the cases have been resolved (NACRO, 1993), the scope for reducing the number of those on remand whom the Courts have not seen fit to detain after sentence is clearly apparent.

Third, the availability of bail produces a series of significant impacts upon the final sentencing decision. Youth justice research has shown just how important the very earliest decisions within the arrest, charge and bail process are in shaping final sentences. Decisions which mark out young people as too difficult or dangerous to be allowed home or transferred to local authority accommodation live with them throughout the process. Views of them are then cast into a particular mould which persists beyond the seriousness of any offences they may have committed or changed information about their circumstances which may subsequently come to light. So it is with bail decisions in the adult court. Not only are defendants remanded in custody faced with additional and significant difficulties in mobilising their defence cases and at high risk of losing those social props – accommodation, work, family contact – which influence Court decisions, they are also identified as 'serious' by the very fact of appearing from custody. In a systemic way, therefore, influencing bail decisions has an impact well beyond the immediate Court hearing.

In this context, the example cited here is of a bail experimental scheme in the far west of Britain, in the South Pembrokeshire area. In rural areas, remote from local prisons, the decisions made at pre-trial and pre-sentence stages have additional impacts upon families and individuals, in terms of separation and contact. The Pembrokeshire scheme is managed by the local Crime Reduction Forum with day-to-day leadership provided by the Probation Service. It aims to provide a supervised bail package for serious and persistent offenders who would otherwise be remanded in custody. A series of criteria determine eligibility for the scheme, designed to ensure that net-widening is avoided. The possibility of inclusion within the scheme is discussed with those defendants who meet the basic criteria. For those who wish to have the option pursued a proposal can then be put before the Court. The scheme subsequently provides for conditional bail, with supervision of those conditions carried out by scheme workers.

Clearly there are a number of important issues which bail schemes have to address if they are not to have unintended and unhelpful consequences. Recent research in another part of South Wales (Hucklesby, 1994) has highlighted a series of these reservations. The proportion of bailees subject to conditional bail has increased steadily since its introduction in 1967. A very large number of restrictive conditions are routinely applied – 33 per cent of conditional bailees in the Hucklesby study were subject to four or more conditions. These conditions are often difficult to reconcile with the personal circumstances of individual bailees or with the grounds of objection to unconditional bail but seem, rather, to be used in a routine or undifferentiated manner. Finally, and most importantly, the view is widely held among those most closely connected with the process that rather than replacing custody, conditional bail is too often a substitute for unconditional arrangements.

The Pembrokeshire scheme cannot claim to have solved all these dilemmas. What it does provide is an in-built series of criteria which attempt to limit the scheme to genuine cases who would otherwise be in prison and to link the imposition of conditions with an understanding by the Court that these will be supervised and enforced with the provision of practical help during the remand period. That process relies upon written procedures but also upon the active agreement of the different parties who have been involved in establishing and running the scheme. Peter Raynor suggests that for the Probation Service to have an impact upon criminal justice systems a new emphasis will have to be placed upon a series of core qualities. These include a willingness to work attentively with other significant actors and in a way which respects the differing perspectives which these others will hold. It also means being clear about and committed to the particular value system of the Probation Service in seeking to bring about change. Where the Service believes the need for change to exist and has proposals for bringing that change about, the arguments for these alterations have to be presented with confidence from the distinctive value base of the Service itself. Within the South Pembrokeshire scheme the human contact and the helpful and constructive aspects of the available support dominates the assessment of its operation, in the views of workers and consumers alike. But it is the systematic work of the Probation Service, in fostering and supporting the scheme which remains owned and managed by a multidisciplinary forum, which has turned the original idea into practical action.

The importance of Probation Service involvement in multidisciplinary schemes which aim to have an impact upon systems in which its clients get caught up is a theme which emerges on many occasions in this book. The Commentary section which discusses examples of work in the field of health contains further evidence of practical success when such investment is made. Gill Stewart, in her chapter on probation involvement in housing (Chapter 5), makes a plea for the Service to take a lead in developing diversion systems for homeless first offenders. Further examples of this sort of work, already operating in many larger urban areas, can be found in the Safer Cities programme. One of the earlier Probation Service involvements in such schemes took place within the Cleveland Probation Service. The Middlesbrough Safer Cities scheme was launched in 1991; in its first year 61 schemes were funded. Probation involvement helped to ensure that 13 per cent of the project budget was spent on four schemes for offenders and ex-offenders; 24 per cent of the budget was devoted to youth projects targeting those at risk of offending. As the Annual Report of the local Service Community Development Unit puts it 'involvement in multi-agency initiatives enables the Probation Service to contribute to the development of services for Cleveland people while making sure that the needs of offenders are given consideration' (Cleveland Probation Service, 1993: 2).

Finally, this Commentary section points to the importance of developing a systemic approach within criminal justice in working with particularly disadvantaged groups who become caught up within the process. Poverty, as other parts of this book make clear, stands as the single greatest barrier to equality of opportunity for a large and growing number of our fellow citizens. Within the criminal justice system the Fines Courts provide the stage for some of the sharpest and most shocking treatment of the poorest people in our society. Failure to meet a financial penalty imposed by the Courts brings severe penalties. The burgeoning use of firms of bailiffs to enter the homes and seize the goods of families who have no hope of replacing the most basic of material possessions is a searing scandal in a rich society. The use of custody for fine default has risen steadily over the past four years. Between 1990 and 1993 the numbers gaoled for default rose by 36 per cent. The length of sentence served has also risen with 38 per cent of those sentenced receiving terms of more than four weeks. These are individuals, let it be recalled, for whom the Court had originally thought custody to be inappropriate. Included in their number, for example, are those people gaoled for that threat to the public safety represented by not having a television licence! Numbers here rose by 110 per cent between 1991 and the end of 1993. Penalties for television licence evasion also fall very heavily on women. While in overall terms only 5 per cent of those sentenced for fine default in February 1994 were women, females made up 36 per cent of those received into custody following failure to obtain a television licence (NAPO, 1994b). Here is a quadruple jeopardy. Women become responsible for television licence evasion because they are more likely to be at home when detector vans call. They are less likely to be able to pay fines subsequently imposed because of the concentration of poverty among women. Because of the further concentration of that poverty among women with children or other caring responsibilities, the consequences of even brief imprisonment will be all the harsher. The process by which this will have come about will be among the most careless of basic principles, for many of the steps along the way to imprisonment will have taken place without the person concerned being present or being represented.

There are at least two sorts of intervention which the Probation Service could attempt to bring about in order to have an influence upon this wicked and wasteful process. First, there are changes to the whole system which would affect all defendants. The Unit Fine scheme was, of course, one such measure. The Probation Service ought to be in the forefront of pressure to have the basis of that system reintroduced by a different Government. There are Parliamentary steps to limit the powers of the Court so as to allow committal to prison for default only in those cases where the original offence was imprisonable. Before then there are steps which could be taken within the present framework. Morris and Gelsthorpe, for example, finding that the supposed last-resort of suspended committals were, in fact, used very early in the process in as many as 50 per cent of the cases they examined, suggested that Arrears Courts should 'be obliged to show that they have used all other power available to them before resorting to suspended committals' (Morris and Gelsthorpe, 1990: 171). There is no reason why, following Peter Raynor's argument that Probation Services should seek to make greater use of their persuasive powers, such a strategy should not be developed and promoted at local level.

A second set of interventions in this area could seek to establish systems which ensure proper services for people within the current way of working. In a Service committed to keeping people out of custody and to building up pro-social behaviour, it is hard to reconcile these aims with the continuing low status of Fines Court work and the withdrawal from active involvement in this forum which is characteristic of present practice. As the number of people received into custody for fine default has risen since 1990, so the number of Money Payment Supervision Orders has fallen year-on-year since 1989. The capacity exists for worthwhile and imaginative schemes which would have real impact upon this neglected but hard-biting area, be it bread and butter arrangements to identify and interview those at risk in the Fines Court in order to intervene on their behalf, or more imaginative schemes such as those in Coventry which draw in the local Citizens Advice Bureau, probation officers and court clerks to examine the cases of those in danger of defaulting. Even the shortest period of imprisonment can have the most substantial consequences. The loss of accommodation, property or employment creates a series of new obstacles which the Probation Service then devotes considerable resources to attempting to overcome. Even money borrowed from unscrupulous lenders to pay off fines will have a harmful effect where budgets are already precariously balanced. Investment in systems which attempt to prevent these outcomes, rather than deal with their consequences, has been the theme of this chapter. We hope the practical examples set out here show how, with imagination and persistence, effective work of this sort is still possible for determined Probation Services.

3 Poverty

Jon Arnold and Bill Jordan

In her excellent book *Penal Policy and Social Justice* (1993), Barbara A. Hudson draws attention to the shift all over the advanced capitalist world, but perhaps most obviously in Britain and the United States, from a social justice to a criminal justice approach to public policy. Starting from her experiences (as a research officer for a probation service) of everyday racial discrimination and the severe penalisation of vulnerable individuals by the court system, she goes on to analyse the dominance of penological thinking over welfare thinking in present-day governance and practice:

> the poor, the disturbed, the migrant, disadvantaged ethnic minorities are consistently over penalised and over imprisoned . . . [We] also see that problem events are more likely to be seen as crime-events rather than illness-events or social needs-events . . . England and Wales, the USA and to a lesser extent Western European countries have . . . prioritised criminal justice policy and expenditure over other spheres . . . In spite of everything probation officers know about the structural problems facing their 'clients' and the consequent need for help, they have largely jettisoned their social work ethos and taken on the juridical ethos. (Hudson, 1993: 3, 5, 11)

Her book is therefore as much a critique of local criminal justice practice as it is of central government policy: there has been a general drift towards a law and order perspective on social relations, and within the court system itself towards ideas of justice proportional to the offence ('just deserts'). Ironically, as Hudson points out, this dominant penal principle makes no claim to effectiveness in crime reduction. This is fortunate for its advocates, since crime rates and prison populations have risen relentlessly while this theory has held sway.

It is all very well for two middle-aged academics, whose probation practice was in the 1960s and 1970s, to start this chapter with such a ringing indictment of current policy and methods. We can imagine that the first response of practitioners reading our opening paragraphs will be along the following lines:

1   The 'golden age' of probation was built on 'success' with far less serious offenders than those with whom the Service is working today.
2   Evidence that welfare-orientated practice changed offending behaviour or reduced crime was scant.
3   The present context for practice is hard-nosed; it must justify its efficiency and effectiveness. Even if practitioners want to help their clients, they are not managed in such a way as to allow this. At best, they can do it only surreptitiously, by stealth.
4   The overall context of practice is hostile to a needs-orientated approach. Many of the supportive resources and facilities that existed in the 1970s are no longer available.
5   Although it is 'obvious' that crime is linked to social deprivation, Government ideology and policy are directed towards denying these links, and legislation and regulation point practice away from the relief of material needs or the provision of tangible support.

Our starting point is an acknowledgement of and respect for all these points, especially points 4 and 5. We aim to take seriously both the criticisms of the earlier era of probation practice, and the ideas and policies that have informed the changes of the 1980s and 1990s. However, we will show that they are fatally flawed, even in terms of the theory on which they are based. Indeed, we will draw heavily on the theoretical underpinnings of recent penology – microeconomics, rational choice theory and game theory – to show that the whole enterprise of institutional reform (of which the criminal justice system itself was a small part) is already a demonstrable failure. We will conclude with some suggestions about ways forward from where we are now.

The central message of this chapter can be very simply stated. We would argue that today's probation clients are not essentially different people from the ones that we supervised in the 1960s and 1970s: indeed, they are quite likely to be their sons and daughters. But their situation is very much worse than their parents' was. They are much less likely to have a job, and much less likely to have access to adequate resources and services for a secure, healthy lifestyle in the mainstream of society. They are far more likely to suffer deprivation and exclusion. Furthermore, and in direct reaction to this deterioration in their life chances compared with those of their parents' generation, they are much more likely to follow strategies that include theft, violence and fraud (including benefit fraud), and to use drugs, as resistance to or compensation for these adversities. In other words, they are not different people, but people in much more desperate circumstances, who have therefore resorted to more desperate measures.

In the context of a fivefold rise in crime during that period, the Probation Service is now working with people who have committed five times as many (and sometimes more serious) offences as the typical caseload of our day. But they do not merit the wholly offence-focused, containment-orientated, technocratic, negative approach that constitutes the official version of practice, and it will not be effective in changing their behaviour.

To practise well in current circumstances needs more imagination, more determination and more willingness to take risks than in our day (Jordan, 1990). But success depends on factors quite other than those that make up the new standards and guidelines. It must do more than we had to do to foster trust, goodwill and credibility in the eyes of clients. It must offer more and better support to sustain cooperation. It must be more creative about resources, more accessible and flexible, if it is to expect reciprocity from its clientele. And it must be more skilled in public relations, mediation and accounting for itself to all those who have an interest in its activities.

The changed climate

Why has public policy – in every sphere, not just criminal justice itself; and in almost every country, not just the ones that elected New Right governments in the 1980s – prioritised law and order over social welfare? Why have Sweden and the Netherlands imprisoned more people, and for longer, as well as Greece and Spain?

One explanation that is popular with sociologists is that modern, complex societies are moving towards a new disciplinary mode ('the carceral archipelago') involving the invasion of every sphere of social life by processes of coercion and restriction (Foucault, 1977). Governments' expert regulation of nineteenth-century societies, based on the total institution (panopticon, asylum, etc.) is extended into the whole polity, as symbolised by electronic tagging, home-based custody, etc. Workfare – compulsory training or labour in exchange for benefits – as pioneered in the United States could be seen as a kind of extension into the provision of public assistance of these carceral systems. It is not that punishment and control have replaced social protection in the new era, but that social provision has taken on a conditional, restrictive, controlling or punitive aspect (Parton, 1994). It is easy to link themes in new-style probation practice – more accurate assessment, designing packages of individualised training or penalties, managerialism –

with similar themes in health and community care. There is a kind of Benthamite convergence between penal policy and the rest of social policy around surveillance, rationing and the control of deviant behaviour (Jordan, 1992).

Although these perspectives are useful, they do not seem to us sufficient to explain the phenomena at issue. It should not be forgotten that the whole 'justice' approach – proportional penalties, 'just deserts' – was a reaction against the unintended consequences of welfarism in juvenile sentencing. For decades in the USA, and throughout the 1970s in Britain, attempts to combine measures to reform or resocialise young offenders with penalties for their wrongdoing had produced perverse outcomes. Instead of reducing custody they had greatly increased its use (Tutt, 1978). In the name of care and concern for youngsters, it had accelerated their progress into the equivalents of approved schools and secure units. The 'justice' movement was as much an attempt to correct these policy failures as to introduce a new system of social control – and the movement produced an impressive research literature (Thorpe *et al.*, 1980) to show its success in reducing incarceration.

Decarceration was also a major theme of adult criminal justice policy, even though it was more concerned with replacing custody by community penalties than with diversion or the avoidance of net-widening. The aim has been to assess 'dangerousness' (Bottoms, 1977), and distinguish between really serious offenders and those in the lower or middle range of criminality, for whom non-custodial penalties may be appropriate. The result has been a process of 'bifurcation' (Hudson, 1993). While the aim of 'twin tracking' in Britain and elsewhere has been to reduce the number of short-term prison sentences, the attempt to identify and 'incapacitate' dangerous and serious offenders by longer sentences (de Haan, 1990) has increased prison populations, even in countries with strong traditions of decarceration, such as the Netherlands.

We must therefore look outside the criminal justice system itself for an analysis of why criminal justice came to be prioritised over social justice. The explanation lies in the loss of faith in social democratic institutions (the welfare state, the social services, and especially the income maintenance systems that were set up in the postwar period) as sources of social order. Even in those countries which have made fewest institutional changes (the Nordic states, Germany) there has been a marked growth in 'new poverty' among the long-term unemployed, young people and single parents (Marklund, 1992). In the face of global economic forces, nation states have either – as in these cases – failed to sustain social protection for these vulnerable groups, or (as in Britain and the USA) actively withdrawn support. At the same time, they have relied on surveillance, rationing and punishment to control these groups, who no longer have a stake in the social democratic order of 'full employment' and social insurance.

But these developments, which have in most European countries been consequences of policy drift, have been enthusiastically justified by New

Right theorists and politicians in Britain and the United States. In the next section we will address the ideological basis of the shift towards criminal justice, and the critique of social justice that underpinned it. We will then go on to evaluate the outcomes of programmes for 'lean welfare' and 'just deserts', using the methodology and theoretical framework with which the New Right attacked the social democratic system.

Crime as rational action

The distinguishing feature of American and British political culture is liberal individualism – a tradition that has been recognisable in Britain since the thirteenth century. The reassertion of property rights and individual responsibilities that was the central thrust of the Reagan–Thatcher era has influenced continental European countries, despite their different (corporatist, Christian Democratic) traditions. The analysis of crime as rational action by individuals in a competitive, market-like situation, and the policy programme this promoted, has gained influence as faith in social democratic institutions declined, and fear about an excluded 'underclass' (or migration and its consequences) grew.

Liberal individualism's hallmark is its central concern with citizens as autonomous actors in a market economy and a competitive, pluralistic form of political organisation (Offe and Preuss, 1990). The institutions of the state should, on this analysis, promote the competencies of such individuals to engage in economic and political activities in pursuit of their interests as independent and responsible beings. In the corporatist tradition, by contrast, state institutions are seen as enabling citizens with potentially conflicting interests to form a general will for the common good: most postwar constitutions and political systems sought to do this through agreements between governments, employers and organised labour (Newman, 1981).

The New Right's critique of the welfare state was that it made citizens less competent as market actors, and encouraged them to pursue strategic political action through the state (Hayek, 1973, 1976). This applied to welfare professionals (like teachers and social workers) as well as to claimants and clients: the public sector protected its denizens from economic realities (there were no pay-offs for effectiveness and efficiency) and encouraged them to maximise their returns from political pressure (to expand the social services, seeking more resources). The only way to require them to acquire these competencies was to restrict opportunities for strategic gains by claimants and clients, by changing the rules of entitlement to benefits and services, and to make the public sector more like a marketplace, by imposing systems that required managers and professionals to compete for resources (Minford, 1984).

The positive part of this programme – 'the property-owning democracy' – was an attempt, by radical institutional reform, to create conditions in which it was rational for individuals to work hard, save, accumulate property, and take responsibility for each other in households. The aim was therefore to improve the pay-offs from enterprise, initiative, thrift, investment and mutuality among family members, as well as to reduce those for dependence on public sector benefits and services. This new social order would be 'spontaneous and self-enforcing' (Hayek, 1976) in the sense that no actor would be able to do better by adopting another strategy, given the strategies of others: everyone would do best by working hard to provide for each other in families.

Thus the role of the state shifted from one of protecting all citizens from economic exploitation or misfortune (the social democratic era) to one of upholding free contracts between autonomous individuals. In the reformed institutional structure, the focus of law was therefore changed from giving positive rights to benefits and services to providing a 'neutral' framework of rules for rational individual choices, among citizens who were assumed to be equal in all relevant respects. An important part of this framework was criminal justice: the law sought to limit opportunities for the predation of property and persons.

In the theory on which this programme rested – rational choice and public choice – criminals are treated as economic actors who calculate the costs and benefits of crime and law-abiding behaviour (Cornish and Clarke, 1986). The whole aim was to set the price of crime high enough to deter all but the reckless and incompetent, but to keep penalties sufficiently 'community based' to avoid excessive costs to the taxpayer. All this fitted the 'justice model' extremely well (Hudson, 1993). It implied that some criminals – professionals and 'dangerous', serious offenders – might be determined, organised or mad enough to require heavy penalties as the 'price' of crime, but others would be influenced by a tariff of less expensive punishments. This approach was well reflected in the Criminal Justice Act 1991.

Unfortunately for the British Government, its calculations and predictions proved to be dramatically wrong, because of the unintended consequences of its policies in other spheres. The Thatcher regime's strategy was to create a free market in labour, with far wider divergence between top and bottom earnings. To do this, it had first to break the power of the trade unions (the Miners' and Printers' strikes of the mid-1980s), then to deregulate the labour market (removing minimum wages and laws forbidding exploitative contracts), and then to reduce direct taxation on earnings (imposing expenditure taxes like VAT instead). Finally, the aim was to focus benefits on the poor (more 'targeted', means-tested systems, less universal, national insurance benefits) and to reduce perverse incentives (that made people better off by claiming, by earning less, or by breaking up their marriages) in the benefits system (Parker, 1982). But these policies have proved to be incompatible with the aim of a 'self-enforcing' order of 'property-owning democracy'. The labour market in many deprived areas has collapsed completely.

While overall 'official' unemployment has fluctuated around 10 per cent since the early 1980s, this has only been achieved by statistical manipulation. Regular, full-time employment (especially for men) has declined relentlessly, and scarcely recovered, even at the height of the 'jobs miracle'. For example, between November 1986 and November 1987, government-measured unemployment among males fell by 750,000, yet the figures for *employment* (including part-time work) for men increased by only 100,000. During the same period, 'self-employment' (mainly consisting of bits and pieces of low-paid service work) increased by 200,000. The rest – the missing 450,000 – disappeared from the statistics, or reappeared in figures for increased claimants of invalidity or disability benefits. With each recession, the number of secure, decently-paid full-time employments declines, with corresponding rises in irregular, part-time, low-paid, subcontract, temporary and agency work, and in long-term unemployment, especially in pockets of concentrated disadvantage (Jordan, 1987, 1989).

For people with few skills, and hence low-earning power, for residents in these disadvantaged areas, and for those who suffered labour-market discrimination (especially young black people), these developments seriously altered the balance sheet between official work and illegal activity. On the one hand, both access to and rewards from official employment declined sharply. On the other, opportunities and pay-offs for all kinds of unofficial activity (undeclared work for cash, dealing, street crime) rose. Ironically, the ultimate 'deregulation' was a situation in which employers and traders could gain considerable advantage from unofficial cash transactions (no questions asked), as could their workers, suppliers and customers. In the name of 'flexibility', the government had achieved such a radical casualisation of work that it actively promoted illegal activity. It had created an environment in which many actors' best strategy was to claim means-tested benefits, and to supplement these with money from undeclared cash work or crime (Jordan and Redley, 1994).

The 'moral panic' in 1993 over rising crime rates, the alterations to the Criminal Justice Act 1991, and the subsequent rise in the prison population, must all be understood in this context. 'Back to basics' was a recognition that Thatcherism had failed – in its own terms. The Government had been largely impervious to accusations that its substitution of criminal justice for social justice was hypocritical and unjust. But it was extremely vulnerable to the increasing evidence – most dramatically evinced by the murder of Jamie Bulger – that the property owning democracy was not a self-enforcing system of social order. Back to basics was a belated and clumsy attempt to provide a readymix morality as the cement for society because its own analysis of crime as rational action showed that its new institutional system did not work. Its hubris in claiming to have established a 'spontaneous order', based on sound juridical principles, had been overtaken by the nemesis of a law-and-order backlash.

In the next section we will address the detail of the Government's legislation on poverty and its relief, to show how the same rationale has contributed to its problems. However, this in turn makes constructive practice in the Probation Service much more difficult.

Poverty and enforcement

In the liberal individualist tradition of the New Right, poverty is not a problem, pauperism is. Poverty is a necessary spur, that drives the poor to work hard, and some of them to improve their condition, while the rest benefit from the general rise in living standards.

In the USA, these principles contributed to an influential critique of the welfare system, that appealed directly to nineteenth-century versions of liberalism. The poor were being pauperised by public assistance, because it rewarded dependence, fecklessness, idleness, improvidence and economic incompetence (Murray, 1984, 1990). Not only was welfare too generous, it was also too unconditional (Mead, 1986). To remoralise and 'reintegrate' the pauperised underclass they should be required to do compulsory training or public service work. Those too recalcitrant to do so should have their benefits withdrawn.

It is ironic that in the USA this critique has been applied almost exclusively to means-tested public assistance schemes (such as Aid to Families with Dependent Children). Social insurance schemes such as unemployment benefits, disability benefits and retirement pensions have emerged largely unscathed from the Reagan–Bush era, while means-tested locally-administered income support has been slashed. But in Britain the same ideas have been taken up by governments that have cut back national insurance benefits (and especially unemployment benefit, which will be abolished altogether in 1996) in favour of the very means-tested systems against which Mead, Murray and their associates have been campaigning. Between 1979 and 1993, expenditure on means-tested benefits (of which income support is the largest element) rose by 260 per cent in real terms, while expenditure on unemployment benefit fell by 60 per cent (weighted to account for the change in numbers of claimants).

In the period since 1985, a whole series of measures have been introduced to tighten up the administration of benefits. While they fall short of US 'workfare' in their rhetoric and legal powers, the substance of their implementation is much the same. Benefits were withdrawn from 16 and 17 year olds; in effect, this enforced participation in Youth Training Schemes (YTS), however poor or irrelevant the training. (Ironically, since one exception to the rule that disallows these young people is a probation condition of residence, crime provides a strategic alternative to homelessness and destitution for many youngsters turned out by their parents for refusing or leaving YTS and losing benefits.)

For adults, they were required first to demonstrate 'availability for full-time employment', and then that they were 'actively seeking work', through various new processes of investigation. These processes were unsubtly linked with new schemes (job clubs, Restart, Employment Training, etc.) to promote active job search and sustain working habits among growing numbers of long-term unemployed claimants. The period of disqualification for unemployment benefit has been increased from six weeks to six months. Despite very limited evidence of the cost-effectiveness of these measures, the Government has continued to move in these directions – as symbolised by its adoption of the term 'Job Seekers' Allowance' for the system to replace unemployment benefit. Behind these measures there has been another struggle that has reinforced the factors analysed in the previous section.

Attempts to screen out claimants who have little intention of getting regular employment (because they will be little or no better off than they are while claiming) are expensive to administer (for example, employing 'industrial psychologists' to interview applicants for benefits). They also take a considerable time to complete. In public choice terms, this means that *transaction costs* rise for the agency and the claimant (who must exist on reduced benefits or no benefits while investigations take place). But this has unintended consequences. A research study on low-income couples found that they used the unfairnesses of delays in payments and suspensions of benefits as reasons for not declaring cash work. They preferred to 'take a chance' by doing short-term or one-off cash-in-hand jobs, because of the penalties they otherwise suffered (getting into debt or rent arrears). Similarly, delays in assessment for family credit put many off taking low-paid jobs (Jordan *et al.*, 1992).

The factors mentioned in the previous section – falling wages and reduced employment security as well as increased casualisation and unemployment – contributed to a 'vicious circle', recognised by the respondents in our research. The struggle over transaction costs (benefits staff trying to pass these on to claimants by delays and suspensions, claimants trying to get the agency to bear them by doing undeclared cash work) created an escalating spiral of mutual mistrust – more fraud investigations, greater hostility towards staff, and so on. As the labour market became more fragmented, so Government measures to drive poor people into low-paid work increased *enforcement costs*. The 'workfare' proposal would exemplify this problem:

measures to enforce low-quality training or low-productivity work are expensive to run, and unless there are better-paid and more secure jobs available for 'trainees' or 'employees' who 'graduate', they solve nothing. The whole system either becomes one of mass occupational therapy or – in its more coercive aspects – a version of Soviet-style state employment, ironically resembling the old communist regime in its inefficiency, unpopularity and anti-liberal character.

Our argument is that all these features 'criminalise' the income maintenance system, both by pushing claimants into bending the rules – practices that they justify in the name of *fairness* – and by then enforcing low-paid work and rationing benefits coercively. They contribute to a political discourse of mistrust and conflict over income maintenance. The Government's welfare policies have done much to create and foster the very 'underclass' attitudes and practices that they claim to combat, by ensnaring a group of long-term claimants in passive, excluded roles, and denying them dignity and value as citizens. Social policy analysts tend to focus on the inadequacy of the rates of benefits, on low take-up, and on loss of rights to discretionary payments (Walker, 1994). It seems to us that these administrative and legal features, that shift income maintenance towards criminal justice and discount social justice, are of at least equal significance.

It is doubly ironic that the political and moral theory that has underpinned these developments has given rhetorical priority to individual liberty. Historically, the branch of liberal theory that emphasises property rights and personal security (the liberalism of Locke, Defoe, Bentham, Malthus, Herbert Spencer and Sir Keith Joseph) has insisted that the state should ration and coerce claimants for the protection of the majority and to 'remoralise' them into submissive poverty. The more optimistic, positive and collectivist liberalism of John Stuart Mill, T.H. Green and Sir William Beveridge (in which the Probation Service had its historic roots) puts a value on citizenship as membership, and on the possibility of growth and change within social relations of trust and mutual respect. The best liberal justification for a generous approach to income maintenance is that poor people cannot be truly autonomous and competent economic and political actors, because they lack the skills and material resources. Thus systems for preventing poverty should aim to provide a decent minimum on which citizens can build (to paraphrase Beveridge), rather than trapping claimants in roles of resentful, excluded supplication.

Under present economic and social conditions, it is increasingly doubtful whether social insurance systems can achieve these goals (Jordan, 1987; Commission on Social Justice, 1993). Radical measures – such as the Basic Income (or Citizens Income) principle (Parker, 1989; Van Parijs, 1992) – may be necessary to give women, young people, black people and people with disabilities the equal autonomy that is the supposed badge of liberal democracy. But in the meantime, probation officers must practice in the mess described by this and the previous section. In the final part of this chapter, we make some suggestions about directions for practice.

Practice in the new context

There are many ironies about the outcomes of the great Thatcher social experiment in Britain. One of them is that, in trying to discredit socialism, her regime largely discredited government itself. As the poll tax revolt showed (for the first time since the War) the people could bring down a prime minister by direct action (democracy by non-compliance, people veto-power). John Major's hapless, inept government has stumbled around in the pitfalls that her systems created (not least rising crime rates), and it has dug some of its own (including the 'back to basics' moral labyrinth in which it fumbled in 1993 and 1994). But in some perverse and unintended ways it has extended liberty and the scope for autonomous action, in sections of society where one would least expect this.

Nostalgia for social democracy tends to cloud perception of its many flaws, especially in the 1970s. Full employment and social protection were constructed around assumptions (about men and women, black and white citizens, insiders and outsiders) that were far from free and equal in their implications. There was nothing particularly edifying or fulfilling in the jobs done by postwar industrial employees, or public service bureaucrats, and little to commend the roles of housewives, carers and low-paid service workers on which these depended. The hurricanes of Thatcherism blew many of these injustices away; the great empty spaces it created provide scope for building new forms of cooperation, based on different social relations. Informally, unofficially, and largely invisibly, some of these processes have started.

The Probation Service now finds itself in much the same double bind as the Government over poverty and crime. If our analysis, schematic and ideal-typical as it necessarily is in a chapter of this length, is accepted as a possible model for explaining this bind, the following conclusions follow:

1   The Service is at the cutting edge of a policy thrust towards 'criminalising' poverty and the poor, of which the Courts are but one instrument.
2   If offenders are in any sense the rational actors that current penological theory constructs them as being, then the strategies which current institutional rules prescribe as unlawful are also 'best replies' (Lyons, 1992) to the actions of those same Government agencies.

3   Offenders have no reason to trust probation officers. Their best strategy is superficial, instrumental cooperation with those aspects of 'offending behaviour programmes' that are consistent with their major strategy (i.e. opportunistic crime and benefit fraud).
4   Conventional 'welfare rights work' (i.e. attempts to use the employment services, benefits agencies and 'normal channels' of interagency coopera-tion) to improve clients' welfare are likely to be counterproductive, since these agencies are increasingly part of a restrictive, punitive and coercive 'criminal justice nexus'. Increased contact runs the risk of provoking a worsening of the offender's situation, and hence an escalation of 'resis-tance' (i.e. crime).

This stark summary deliberately overstates the case, rather in the manner that the New Right used the same intellectual tools to vilify the social demo-cratic system. But if it delineates a nightmare version of the Probation Service's dilemma, it also clarifies why the methods prescribed by the Home Office cannot possibly work. To confront offending behaviour by crude juxtaposition of offence and penal consequences, even to 'educate' about some of the less obvious longer-term consequences of crime (for others and victims), scarcely addresses the problem. If lawful behaviour pays as little as it does under the British Government, crime does not have to pay much to be a rational strategy. If Government policy in every sphere treats the poor as calculative criminals, and devises its rules and procedures accordingly, their best strategic principle is always to act as if every public agency is out to cheat, restrict or punish them, and to look for ways of turning these systems against their authors.

Crime, of course, almost always takes this form; it thrives on attempts to thwart it. Nothing provides more fertile ground for crime than 'security'. Credit card theft and fraud, the major growth sector, illustrates how the 'security' of not using cash has backfired. Honest citizens feel safer in cars than walking in the street, yet car crime easily outstrips muggings, offering far richer pickings. Our favourite example was the ingenious thief who put up a notice at the relevant point of his (or her) local bank saying, 'Night safe out of order; please use temporary night safe', and then pocketed the contents of the conveniently large-opening letter box that had been labelled 'tempo-rary night safe'. In much the same way, 'offending behaviour programmes', with their ideology of optimistic consequentialism, can easily be turned on their heads, to reveal exactly what they purport to disprove: crime may not always pay, but it is rather more reliable than the official alternatives.

Suppose that practice were instead to start at the other end of the problem. Instead of trying to persuade offenders that they would do better to obey and trust the law, the Government, employers and the DSS, suppose it asked them whom they do trust. We suspect that all but the most desperate and vulnerable few would be able to think of (if not necessarily to name to their probation officers) a few trusted friends. Suppose that, instead of trying to weaken these links and networks, or isolate the individual in the name of resocialisation, practice were to be directed towards strengthening and resourcing them, channelling them into activities that had clear pay-offs, in terms of the quality of members' lives.

Of course, much of this is old hat – taken for granted practice wisdom. It forms the basis of groupwork and project work in every probation team. Yet current Home Office orthodoxy pulls in the opposite direction towards artificial rather than 'natural' groups, based on existing social networks; towards purposeful, offence-focused work, rather than activity which produces valued goods or is a good in itself. In so far as this old tradition survives, it does so in spite of, rather than because of, the new orthodoxies of 'just deserts' and confronting offending behaviour.

Next to crime and benefit fraud, informal cooperation, mutual aid and networking have probably been the greatest growth areas in the bombed-out aftermath of Thatcherism. Although by definition little measurement was possible, the authors of the Exeter research study were very impressed by the evidence of extensive systems of mutual support, and rather sophisticated bartering networks (for do-it-yourself building, and trade in birds, fish and animals) in the deprived community researched (Jordan *et al.*, 1992: Ch. 7). Voluntary agencies have gone with the grain of these developments (Drakeford, 1990), and such organisations as credit unions and cooperatives have sought to create new collective resources in devastated communities (Holman, 1989). We would argue that probation practice should start to move back in this direction, rather than isolating itself in office-based monitoring and formalised, offence-focused work.

The problem of what young unskilled males should do with their lives in modern societies is far more general and fundamental than the issues raised by offending behaviour programmes. All over the developed world, there is little constructive role for such citizens, and their contribution to the formal economy and organised social systems is frustrated and blocked. In an absolutely general sense, unless they can be enabled, encouraged and given some resources to organise *themselves* in meaningful, constructive activities of their own choosing, they will inevitably become the predators on the edges of the grazing herds of property-owning democrats. The deeply offensive image of young criminals as hyenas is a self-fulfilling prophecy: given no other role, that is what they will become. The Probation Service should be in the vanguard of those seeking to support the self-organising, self-defining, self-respecting action of such people. Some services for the parents of children in need are beginning to work in this way, albeit mainly with women. Considering how far they had to move from the statutory, coercive, abuse-focused approaches of the 1970s and early 1980s, to these practices based on

partnership (Children Act, 1989, Regulations and Guidance), it is not too ideal-
istic to ask the Probation Service to initiate some moves in the same direction.

Conclusion

This chapter is an attempt to provide an analysis of the material context of
probation practice, focusing on the conceptual links between poverty and
crime. It deliberately sets out to be shocking, by deserting the conventional
terms of this rather sterile debate – the poor as victims of Government policy,
offenders as misguided or evil-minded members of this oppressed group,
who turn against their own, and need to be redirected, courtesy of the DSS,
benefit agency, employment service and labour market, back into the mainstream. In our view, that analysis provides a hopeless guide to practice;
indeed, it does little or nothing to challenge offending-behaviour orthodoxies. If practitioners believe that there is a high road, via YTS, ET, family credit
and a nice little job, back to the comfortable mainstream, they are likely to be
enthusiastic advocates of 'just deserts', and to have about as much credibility
with their more vulnerable clients as would a Home Office spokesperson.

We have argued that the law and policy that direct the work of poverty
relief are now cast in a criminal justice mould, and that this orientation is
bound to increase because the deregulated market economy cannot deliver
the kind of employment for unskilled workers that gives them the basis for a
stake in society. Accordingly, stricter enforcement of more conditional and
restrictive benefit regulations will escalate mistrust and conflict between
claimants (irregular low-paid workers as well as long-term beneficiaries) and
systems of public administration. Thus there will be increasing similarities in
the ethos and methods, and in the social relations, of income maintenance
and criminal justice agencies. Anyone who doubts this could usefully spend
some time comparing an average day of an employment trainee in a low-skill
scheme with one spent on a community service programme, or a Restart
group with an offending behaviour group. Which of each pair has the higher
failure rate, we wonder.

Yet the picture is not hopeless, once the dead-end thinking of proportional
justice and workfare is abandoned – and even within one of the stupidest
governments since Lord North's there are some ministers with glimmers of
insight. For example, the 1993 budget did not contain all the expected
measures for crackdown on claimants, and even introduced new features –
especially the child care allowances for single parents – that provide scope
for positive initiatives, if practitioners have the imagination to use these.

Trust and cooperation will be difficult to gain in the context we have
described, but there are some factors in the probation officer's favour, if they

choose to use them. In our long experience, deprived, disadvantaged and even deviant people are remarkably open to approaches that offer them respect and support, and extraordinarily willing to recognise and give credit to genuineness and empathy among good practitioners, even after repeated bad experiences from colleagues and the Service. The same, of course, cannot always be said of the management structure of probation, or of the Home Office, but in a world of galloping failure and spiralling loss of credibility, perhaps courageous innovators hold key advantages, if they are willing to take full responsibility for what they do.

Finally, listening skills have not exactly been at a premium in the era of confronting offending behaviour. However, our experiences (in work and in research) tell us that clients have a great deal to teach professionals about how their communities work, and how they could be helped to work better. All we are suggesting is that practitioners reorientate themselves towards trying to strengthen the positive features of these communities, and providing offenders with the skills and competencies they need to contribute (probably more by informal than formal means) to a better quality of life within them.

Editors' commentary

Primary poverty cannot be conquered by probation officers but the stark facts of poverty dominate probation practice. The financial circumstances in which offenders live are among the most impoverished in an increasingly, and deliberately, unequal society. In a series of core reports commissioned by the Association of Chief Probation Officers, the national deterioration in the social circumstances of probation clients has been vividly traced (Stewart *et al.*, 1989; Peelo *et al.*, 1992; Stewart and Stewart, 1993a). In 1993, the National Association of Probation Officers conducted a survey among its members of the financial circumstances of 1,331 offenders on probation supervision. It discovered that individuals 'commencing probation supervision were 8 times more likely to be unemployed and 2 to 3 times more likely to be long-term unemployed than the rest of the population' (NAPO, 1993: 8). Almost 80 per cent of the whole client population were dependent upon means-tested benefits, compared with 20 per cent of the whole population, rising to more than 90 per cent in major urban areas.

Neither, for Probation Service clients, are these findings confined to abandoned fringes of the post-Thatcher economy. In 1991 the Somerset Service investigated the links between poverty and offending in what the resulting Report called 'a relatively prosperous County' (Hughes, 1991). Even within a deliberately cautious and conservative approach to definitions of poverty and need, 67 per cent of all Service clients in 1990 were living in poverty. A substantial number (137) had no income of any sort. A far larger group (628) were in receipt of a weekly income of less than £92. Only 314, or 29 per cent, were living above the poverty line.

Nor is the experience of poverty equally shared among the different groups of people who come to the attention of probation officers. Women carry the burden of poverty in our society, through their often marginal relationship to the economy and because of the burden of care for dependants which Government policy has forced back into the domestic sphere. Black people, too, because of their over-representation in unemployment and poorly paid, low status occupations are more likely than other groups to be at the sharp end of poverty and material deprivation. In a Commentary which will place most of its emphasis on things which the Probation Service could be doing, but isn't, it is worth noting here that the principle of positive practice in relation to particularly disadvantaged groups can and does form part of present policies in significant parts of the Service. The Inner London Probation Service (ILPS) anti-poverty strategy, for example, has as one of its core beliefs 'that poverty work is at the heart of anti-discriminatory practice. Black people, women, lone parents and people with disabilities are disproportionately represented in the poorer sections of the community. People who are gay or lesbian can face additional difficulties in facing poverty' (ILPS, 1991: 6).

Poverty on this scale provides the essential context for offending. Whether following the social democratic case, or citing the more radical analysis of Arnold and Jordan, the outcome remains the same: poverty results in higher levels of offending. Despite this, however, probation itself is hesitant in its response to these dilemmas. Practical measures to address the difficulties seem either to be outside the scope of what the Service has to offer or beyond the ability of local teams and individuals to design and develop. The Northumbria Service, for example, found that sensitivity among officers to the structural and political nature of poverty was accompanied in 20 per cent of officers interviewed by a belief that the weight of these factors put poverty in the lives of clients beyond the remit or capacity of the Service to influence. As the Northumbria report notes 'this "nothing works" attitude can be damaging and self-limiting' (Northumbria Probation Service, 1994: 21).

This Commentary, and this book, argue that this should not and need not be the case. Programmes which have an effective impact upon offending must tackle the issues most closely allied to it. The same Northumbria survey which found pessimism and despair about the overwhelming nature of poverty also found that 93 per cent of probation officers interviewed felt that poverty to be an important or very important factor linked to offending and as such an essential area of work for the Service. The need for such strategies, moreover, is emphasised because it is assistance in these basic areas which is most valued by Probation Service clients and appreciated by them when it is delivered (see, for example, Stockley *et al.*, 1993). The climate within which the Service currently operates does not easily support the achievement of the trust, goodwill and credibility with clients with which Arnold and Jordan close their chapter. In placing a new priority upon these qualities in practice nothing will be more important than the willingness of Probation Services and officers to intervene in those systems which place money in the pockets of poor people and to develop new services which have a direct impact upon the financial circumstances in which their clients live.

In this Commentary, three distinct strategies are suggested through which, even in these times, workers and agencies can move in this direction. The first, and in some ways the most obvious, is to consider the direct ways in which Probation Services, as powerful organisations in their own right, deploy their financial resources. Social work agencies in general operate within impoverished communities. As such they are in a position – often ignored – to have an impact upon the economies of such localities. Decisions about employment strategies, location of offices, purchase of goods and services all contribute to a pattern in which Services are either net contributors or net subtractors from the amount of money which circulates within a local economy. An organisation which heedlessly develops recruitment policies which determine that its staff have to be drawn almost exclusively from outside such communities, which locates these staff in large and remote office suites and which uses its purchasing power to enrich far-off companies and corporations actually worsens the financial circumstances of those it is meant to assist. In contrast, decisions to invest these resources within such communities stands as a practical and principled symbol of determination to tackle the circumstances which produce such problems in the first place.

In this regard, there are important lessons to be drawn by the Probation Service from the actions of local authority Social Services Departments. The drive to decentralise council services has, in important ways, been driven by anti-poverty strategies which recognise the impact council spending can produce. In South Glamorgan, for example, social work decentralisation has seen the break-up of a large, centrally situated office – at least two bus journeys from the parts of Cardiff in which most clients live – to a pattern of local and neighbourhood centres. The practice basis for this change is most often expressed in terms of partnership, accessibility and sensitivity to local needs. In economic terms, however, the change is also part of the Council's overall anti-poverty programme which positively encourages the direct investment of resources within the most needy communities.

The resources held by Probation Services may not rival the spending power of local authority services. Yet they stand as a source of considerable riches to those without any such facilities. Returning to Northumbria, a Service with a fine record of positive attempts to think about and address poverty issues in its local areas, a series of positive measures can be discovered, from the formal adoption of a Service anti-poverty policy to the appointment of a specialist Debts and Benefits Adviser. Yet, the report on the Northumbria Probation Service's response to disturbances on Tyneside in 1991 (North *et al.*, 1992: 10) notes, as their 'most important reflection on the role of the Probation Service', the retreat which had taken place in its work with disadvantaged communities:

> it has become increasingly apparent in the course of our discussions that gradually and progressively the Service has withdrawn from the community focus which at one time used to characterise its work. Field work in particular is increasingly becoming office based with home visits being almost completely eschewed by some officers . . . The North Shields team have been made to realise how little they actually knew of the Meadowell Estate despite this being the source of 30% of its work. . . . The SPO described his team as being 'physically and in many respect professionally distanced from the issues and concerns affecting the residents of the Meadowell Estate'. (North *et al.*, 1992: 10)

Among the suggested actions highlighted in the report was the re-establishment of a physical presence in the area, if only by means of a reporting centre. Anti-poverty policies, in other words, have to include an audit and a realignment of the spending and service-delivery decisions which lie directly within a Service's own control if they are to be consistent with and complementary to the aim of alleviating the poverty experienced by clients.

The second strand in a strategy for addressing poverty among Probation Service clients lies in a refocusing of work in the basic business of welfare rights. Such a reorientation requires two main ingredients. Arnold and Jordan make a convincing case for the way in which the collapse of the traditional institutions of the welfare state have led to their replacement by policies of rationing and coercion. The conclusion they draw is that attempts to intervene on behalf of clients in these systems is more likely to have damaging than useful consequences. Yet that need not necessarily be so. Intervention with hostile systems which proceeds from a naïve belief in their basic helpfulness, or which place a premium upon the maintenance of 'good relations' between one worker and another or one bureaucracy and another is certainly likely to produce unintended and harmful results. It is not part of the argument of this Commentary to deny the ever-present danger of cosy and collusive relationships developing between professional workers in regular contact, to the exclusion and at the cost of clients. The Probation Service is, in any case, well placed in this regard, for Courtroom practice furnishes some of the worst examples of this process. Here is a procedure ostensibly organised on adversarial principles in order to protect and enhance justice which so often operates according to a far from covert set of comfortable conveniences maintained by insiders to the exclusion of defendants and complainants alike.

The evidence is that probation practice, in some parts at least, has learned these lessons. The Policy Studies Institute study of informal benefit advisers – professional workers who, within their overall duties, routinely provide advice about social security benefits – found that probation officers regarded this work as an integral part of the service provided to clients. While the intention was widespread, however, the delivery of such services was more patchy. The report identified uncertainty on the part of officers about the detail of benefit entitlement, limited access to necessary information and a pattern of active work which depended unduly upon the enthusiasm or otherwise of individual Senior Probation Officers and workers. The report expressly included views from those who believed that pressures to be seen 'tackling offending' were detracting from work in this field (Perkins *et al.*, 1992).

The advent of the Social Fund, with its petty humiliations of claimants, its Russian roulette approach to outcomes and the propulsion of its recipients into debt and despair, acted as a catalyst in reforming attitudes towards benefit advice in some of its aspects. The advice of the Professional Practice Committee of NAPO to workers pursuing Social Fund claims was forthright: priority was to be placed upon 'clients' definition of their own needs', officers were to maintain a clear distinction between their own role as providers of independent advice and assistance by 'not sharing responsibility for the management of the Social Fund with the DHSS' (NAPO, 1988: 4).

The evidence of professional performance in this area contains some encouragement. Among the different research projects set up to investigate the impact and operation of the Social Fund the practice of probation staff was reported upon by, for example, Lancaster University. The central thrust of their findings is to confirm the central flaws of the Social Fund itself while vividly illustrating the shocking impact of its deliberate shortcomings upon the lives of the most disadvantaged probation clients. Against that background it and other studies (Becker and Silburn, 1990; Craig and Glendinning, 1990) also develop two further themes of particular relevance to the purposes of this book.

First, there is clear evidence of widespread and persistent effort on the part of probation officers and social workers in pursing Social Fund claims and general agreement that such intervention was likely to result in beneficial outcomes for their clients. The Joseph Rowntree Foundation, for example, reported that workers 'spend a lot of time and effort in dealing with clients' Social Fund-related problems: at least an hour had already been spent in 64% of cases' producing a result in which 'intervention on clients' behalf seemed to be effective insofar as contact had been made by social workers in the course of 62% of successful grant applications, while there was no contact in 53% of those which were rejected outright' (Rowntree Foundation, 1990: 2). Four years later, and with an ever-diminishing level of help from the Fund, the

National Association of Probation Officers reported that 'the only successes are on appeal and involve probation or other advocacy' (NAPO, 1994a).

Second, the surveys establish that clients themselves were appreciative of effort as well as results, or even where no results were forthcoming. The same Rowntree survey commented that 'clients often had low expectations and were easily pleased with very little' (1990: 3). The Northumbria survey of probation practice on poverty issues also found that 75 per cent of clients who had received such help from a probation officer rated that help as useful or very useful (Northumbria Probation Service, 1994). The second strand in the strategic programme suggested here, therefore, is – unlike Arnold and Jordan – a renewed emphasis on direct intervention with state income maintenance systems, but an intervention which takes the hostility of those systems as its starting point and directs its efforts on behalf of clients in a way which is dedicated to the protection of clients' interests and prepared for the confrontation which might follow.

Finally to the third strand in this Commentary section and the one which is closest to the strategy advanced by the chapter writers. It is our contention that, within some of the most disadvantaged communities, examples already exist of local initiatives which can have a direct impact upon the financial circumstances of those impoverished families and individuals who live within them. These initiatives include: credit unions, debt redemption work, cooperative buying schemes, LETS schemes, self-build initiatives and cooperative employment arrangements. In credit union development, for example, the Greater Manchester Probation Service was involved in an early and successful effort to establish a community-based union in Wigan (Homewood, 1989). The presence of probation staff, together with representatives of other local statutory and voluntary agencies, provided a launch-pad through which people living in the union's area could mobilise, organise and deliver a service which directly improves the financial circumstances of its members. For these initiatives are characterised by principles of self-government and cooperation. They are created and maintained by individuals within some of the most economically abandoned communities, drawing on a resourceful and skilful sense of enterprise which is based both upon resilience and determination together with a clear-eyed understanding of the environment in which they live and the knowledge of how best to bring about necessary improvement in it. There is a real role for social welfare agencies in engendering interest in new initiatives, in helping to untap the potential which can lie hidden in neglected communities and in encouraging, supporting and developing the ideas and practical ventures which emerge. To foster these developments and to bring their benefits to Probation Service clients requires the very qualities which Arnold and Jordan cite – a willingness to seek trust and cooperation and to offer them, in return, a willingness to respect and support the efforts made on the ground and to listen and learn from those who know from their own experience about how their communities work, and how they could be helped to work better. It means as well a recognition that ownership and control of the practical projects which result must remain firmly in the hands of those who participate directly within them. Empowerment may be an idea which is already hackneyed but it lies at the heart of successful intervention in the economic circumstances of poor communities.

In our view the traditional strengths of the Probation Service still allow it to be well placed to work in this way and to secure for its clients the direct financial benefits which these initiatives offer. That these ideas ought to form a more central part of the repertoires of social welfare agencies generally and the Probation Service in particular seems to us to be of central importance to a worthwhile form of practice in a Britain which, in 1995, has more in common with the society of 1895 than 1945. Poverty and crime are intrinsically linked. To have an impact on the one means to attend actively to the other.

4   Employment, training and offending

Iain Crow

Work has long been connected with ways of dealing with crime and criminals, whether it be the use of the Vagrancy Acts of the seventeenth century as a way of controlling the workless and itinerant, or the eighteenth and nineteenth centuries' emphasis on work in prison as a means of rehabilitation. The availability of employment and training opportunities has several implications for offenders and those who have dealings with them. The aspect that has attracted most attention in recent years is the extent to which unemployment may be linked with crime. This has led to other implications receiving much less attention. In addition to any link between unemployment and offending there is the matter of how the criminal justice process deals with unemployed offenders. There is also the question of what employment and training opportunities exist for offenders, and what they achieve. This chapter considers each of these aspects.

Unemployment and crime

Investigating the relationship

Investigating the extent to which unemployment is related to crime involves overcoming several problems. The most immediate of these are the twin problems of determining just how much crime and how much unemployment there is. Those who work in criminal justice agencies are aware that the number of notifiable offences recorded by the police are far from being a true measure of the amount of crime. Nonetheless such officially recorded figures have been used in studies of the relationship between unemployment and crime, not only in this country but elsewhere. Crime recorded by the police can be supplemented with information obtained from victim surveys, such as the British Crime Survey, but this does not overcome the problem since victim surveys also have their limitations. When considering the relationship between crime and unemployment it is not very useful to refer to crime in general. Different types of crime may be affected by economic change in different ways, or not at all. In this regard a distinction is often made at least between property crimes and crimes against the person.

Knowing how much unemployment there is is no easier than measuring how much crime there is, and the basis on which unemployment is counted has changed over the years. The two main methods used tend to give different levels of unemployment, but follow broadly the same trend over time. Just as an overall measure of crime is less helpful than looking at specific offences so, in considering the relationship between unemployment and crime it is useful to look at more specific aspects of employment and unemployment. For example, it is possible that the relationship between unemployment and crime depends more on the level of long-term unemployment than on unemployment overall, and that it is not so much being out of work as the prospects of future employment that matter. The number of people unemployed for more than a year tends to persist after unemployment as a whole has gone down.

Another feature of recent years is the changing nature of employment. Declines in the manufacturing and construction industries may well affect those who are, by virtue of their background and training (or lack of it), most likely to commit offences. Where employment prospects have developed, they have often been in jobs that are short term or part time and, whereas men are more likely to be offenders, women have tended to occupy part-time opportunities proportionately more than men. The social implications of this change in the patterns of employment and the kind of jobs available, particularly in terms of offending patterns, have yet to be fully explored.

While criminal statistics and employment figures may not be absolute measures of either phenomenon, neither are they entirely meaningless. As far as crime is concerned, recorded crime does at least seem to be indicative of trends in the changing rate of crime (Field, 1990: 2; Dickinson, 1994: 18). Having settled on some measures of unemployment and crime, however unsatisfactory, other matters need to be considered. Any change in unemployment rates must precede a change in crime in order for any causal link to exist. Consideration must also be given to the impact of any factors that may affect both employment and crime levels and, as far as possible, these factors must be controlled for. It has been suggested that what is really important is poverty (Gravelle *et al.*, 1981), and unemployment is only one originator of poverty. In recent years it has been suggested that there is a link between unemployment in neighbourhoods with high levels of social deprivation and drug misuse (Dorn and South, 1987), and the connection between drug misuse and crime (Mott, 1989) gives rise to the possibility of a triangular relationship in certain circumstances. Other pitfalls to be avoided include the danger of concluding that, because there is a high proportion of unemployed people among a caseload of offenders, this is sufficient to conclude that the unemployed are more likely to become offenders. To take a slightly more bizarre example, the fact that a high proportion of alcoholics drink tea does not mean that tea-drinkers will become alcoholics. Another pitfall is what is termed the ecological fallacy. Simply because one observes a high level of unemployment in a particular area of high crime, this does not mean that the unemployed are more crime prone: what is true for a group or community does not necessarily apply at the individual level and vice versa (Farrington, 1992). Account may also need to be taken of any changes in law enforcement policy which might affect crime rates at times of high unemployment, such as the tendency to counter economic and ensuing social deprivation by repressive means (UNSDRI, 1976: 21).

Ways of looking at the relationship

Numerous studies have been carried out in several countries examining the relationship between unemployment and crime over varying periods of time. Simply looking at variations in the crime rate alongside the unemployment rate is not, however, very informative. A lot depends on which time periods are chosen. Tarling (1982), for example, looked at variations in the relationship between unemployment and crime for the period 1950–80, and pointed to the fact that during the 1960s unemployment was low, but crime was rising.

While comparisons of crime and unemployment rates over time can look very persuasive they have their limitations. One is the technical problem that the measures of unemployment and crime may change over time, so it is necessary to ensure that the figures are indeed comparable over the period in question. More difficult to overcome is the fact that other things also change over time, such as criminal policy, and these may exert their own effects independently of unemployment. There are two studies in the UK that have looked at groups of young offenders, and have done so by using a technique which is referred to as using each individual as their own control. This involves comparing periods when young people were in work (or otherwise actively engaged, for example in education or training schemes), with periods when they were not in work, and seeing whether offending is more likely to occur in the latter periods than in the former. A study in Northern Ireland in 1980 which used this approach found that young offenders were about twice as likely to commit offences when not engaged in work, education or training as when they were (Gormally *et al.*, 1981). In another study using a similar approach, drawing on data from the Cambridge Study of Delinquent Development, it was found that the rate of offending was about three times as great for individuals experiencing unemployment as it was for those with work (Farrington *et al.*, 1986).

In addition to the research mentioned above, there have been many other studies of the relationship between unemployment and crime, in the UK and elsewhere, some of them going back a number of years. It is not possible to undertake an exhaustive review of the research here, only to summarise some of the more salient features of what has been found.

Economic indicators   The first point to be made is that unemployment is often used to stand as an indicator of economic conditions in general, and when people talk about the relationship between unemployment and crime they may be thinking about the state of the economy as a whole. There are a number of economic indicators, of which unemployment is only one, and it may not even be the most relevant one since it tends to lag behind other indicators. One of the most frequently quoted analyses in the UK in recent years is that by Simon Field of the Home Office Research and Planning Unit. This concluded that, 'economic factors have a major influence on trends in both property and personal crime' (Field, 1990: 5). Field himself questioned whether unemployment adds anything extra to the explanation of any type of crime, and his analysis has been criticised on a number of grounds. However, a Cambridge economist has suggested that looked at in more detail Field's data do indeed show a relationship between the two (Dickinson, 1994); in particular he argues that the relationship only becomes apparent with the onset of mass unemployment, that it links closely to burglary and that it is most apparent within that offence group with young males.

Age   Age is an important factor in the relationship between unemployment and crime for several reasons. First, much of the crime committed by known offenders occurs among the young: almost half (45 per cent) of all known offenders are under 21 years old (Barclay, 1993: 24). Second, unemployment rates are highest among the youngest age groups (Department of Employment, 1993b: Table 2.15). So any link between unemployment and crime is likely to be of particular significance for younger people. A number of studies have considered age in relation to unemployment and crime (Dickinson, 1994; see Crow *et al.*, 1989: 6–10, for further details). This is not a simple task because, for example, account has to be taken of the fact that many younger people are in a transitional phase between the worlds of education and employment and may not be participants in the labour market. The indications from most studies are that, with some qualifications, unemployment is linked with crime trends among young people. Fleisher, for example, concluded that: 'An examination of delinquency rates and other variables by age and through time suggests that the effect of unemployment on juvenile delinquency is positive and significant' (1963: 553).

Gender A noticeable feature of the discussion about unemployment and crime is the rarity of any mention of women. Most of the studies that have been conducted focus on males. There are some understandable (though not necessarily excusable) reasons for this. One is the fact that females make up a relatively small proportion of known offenders, and therefore in a given sample they are likely to form only a small number, making tests of statistical significance impractical. This means additional investigation is needed to incorporate a viable female sample, and the resources available for research investigations are often limited. However, particularly given the changing nature of employment, and the growth in the proportion of female offenders in recent years, there is a strong case for more work to be done on female employment patterns and offending. One exception to this neglect of female employment is a study conducted in Australia. The authors suggested that the notion that unemployment necessarily causes crime has been largely based on analysis of data relating to males, and that high unemployment among females was not mirrored in the female crime figures (Naffine and Gale, 1989).

Race Another important consideration is race. In general unemployment rates are appreciably higher among ethnic minority groups than among whites: 13 per cent compared with 7 per cent over the three year period 1989–91 (Department of Employment, 1993b: Table 10). This remains true even when qualifications are taken into consideration: ethnic minority groups are more likely to be unemployed than whites with similar qualification levels. It is also true when age and gender are considered. Unemployment rates have been highest among the Pakistani/Bangladeshi and West Indian communities, and among 16–24 year olds in each main ethnic minority group. Thus for 16–24 year olds the white unemployment rate in the Labour Force Survey 1989–91 was 8 per cent, whereas for Pakistani/Bangladeshi it was 12 per cent and for West Indian/Guyanese it was 18 per cent.

Since the early 1980s there has been an increasing amount of research on race and criminal justice. This has found not only that ethnic minorities (especially those of West Indian and Guyanese origin) are over-represented at various points in the criminal justice process, but also that black offenders are more likely to be unemployed (Hudson, 1989: 28–9; Hood and Cordovil, 1992: 56–7). One of the conclusions suggested by such studies is that ethnic minority over-representation in the criminal justice process probably has more to do with social class and economic opportunity than with criminality, and that social disadvantage and discrimination is a precursor of any discrimination in criminal justice (see, for example, Cook and Hudson, 1993: 16–17). Despite this, relatively little work has been done in the UK on whether an association between unemployment and crime is evident for particular ethnic groups.

To the extent that there is a relationship between unemployment and crime, an important consideration is whether any increase in crime resulting from higher levels of unemployment is a consequence of people who, but for unemployment, would have otherwise been law abiding, or people who were already likely to offend turning to crime more often. To find the answer to that question it is necessary to turn to studies where employed and unemployed people are compared. There are few such studies, and so far the best indication of the answer in the UK comes from the Cambridge study. This concluded that the latter was the case, 'since the relation with crime was greatest for those who were the most predisposed towards offending. Unemployment, therefore, did not seem to cause basically law-abiding youths to commit crimes' (Farrington *et al.*, 1986: 351).

Unemployment and social instability

Despite the belief of seven out of ten members of the public surveyed in an opinion poll that unemployment is one of the main causes of crime (*Guardian*, 21.3.94), it is clear that the implications of unemployment rates for crime are by no means simple. Much depends on what age, gender and ethnic groups are being considered. There is also evidence that the implications can be indirect as well as direct. For example, unemployment can affect the family and its relationships as well as individuals, and there are indications that high risk of unemployment may be a factor affecting parental supervision, which is related to the likelihood of delinquency (Wilson, 1987: 294). A study in the USA investigated communities with high levels of unemployment, and concluded that unemployment resulted in a destabilising and weakening of community structures. It was suggested that such communities are more at risk of high crime rates (Sviridoff and McElroy, 1985). On the other hand close knit communities with strong social ties may to some extent mitigate a tendency for unemployment to produce adverse social consequences. Some econometric analyses have attempted to calculate the exact extent to which unemployment affects crime rates. Fleisher, for example, estimated that a 100 per cent increase in unemployment over a given period could result in a 25 per cent increase in the delinquency rate, and claimed that if unemployment were to be reduced by half at any one time it would be accompanied by a decline in property crime of approximately 10 per cent (Fleisher, 1963). Such estimates should perhaps be taken as indicating a general direction rather than a mechanical and inevitable formula. While it is reasonable to conclude that unemployment is a factor where crime is concerned, it is much harder to be sure about the precise extent and nature of the relationship, given that crime is also related to many other factors. A reasonable summary of the present state of knowledge seems to be that offered by Dickinson when he says that unemployment is 'a catalyst for those having least educational and economic opportunities' (1994: 32).

Offenders, employment and the criminal process

Turning to look more specifically at offenders, the point has already been made that a high incidence of unemployment among offenders is not itself evidence of a relationship between unemployment and crime. The extent of unemployment among offenders is, however, important to those who deal with them, since it has a significant bearing on what may or may not be done with them. There are no comprehensive figures for the proportion of known offenders who are unemployed, employed, or involved in other types of activity. But it is clear from various studies that those who are known to have offended are substantially more likely to be out of work than the population as a whole. A Home Office study of nine Magistrates' Courts and ten Crown Court centres was undertaken in 1993 to assess the impact of the Criminal Justice Act 1991. This found that of 3,600 persons sentenced during January and February 1993, 70 per cent were unemployed, 18 per cent were employed and 4 per cent were in full-time education or training schemes (House of Commons Official Report (Hansard), 7 February 1994, Cols 25–6). A national prison survey undertaken by the Home Office found that just prior to imprisonment about a half were working (51 per cent); by the time release dates were reached, however, only about one-sixth of prisoners said they actually had a job to go to (Walmsley *et al.*, 1992).

From time to time various Probation Services have produced information on the extent of unemployment among those who form their workload. A more systematic attempt to monitor the employment status of offenders coming to the attention of Probation Services has been developed by the Association of Chief Officers of Probation (ACOP). Of 30,463 offenders on whom officers prepared pre-sentence reports during the period January to June 1993, 70 per cent were registered unemployed, 20 per cent were in employment and 4 per cent were in education or training (ACOP, 1993). A survey undertaken by the National Association of Probation Officers (NAPO) in 1993 involved a sample of 1,331 people drawn from 19 cities and rural areas who were the subject of criminal supervision in England and Wales. It was found that 55 per cent of those under probation supervision had been unemployed for more than 12 months. At the time of the survey one-third of all unemployed persons in England and Wales were long-term unemployed, whereas in the sample just over two-thirds (67 per cent) of those who were unemployed were long-term unemployed. In Newcastle, Liverpool and Birmingham over 80 per cent of the probation caseload were long-term unemployed, and it is suggested that, 'This has tremendous implications for planning, crime prevention and caseload management' (NAPO, 1993: 9). Despite the fact that these investigations have taken place in a variety of contexts and for different purposes, a fairly consistent picture of high levels of unemployment among offenders emerges.

Much has been written about unemployment in relation to the sentencing of offenders. High levels of unemployment among those in prison are not proof that the unemployed are sentenced more severely. Account has to be taken of intervening factors, especially the nature of the offence and previous record. However, there has been consistent evidence of a relationship between unemployment and the prison population. This relationship has been observed in several Western countries and found to persist over a period of time (Brenner, 1976a, 1976b; UNSDRI, 1976: 14). One obvious possible explanation for this is that if higher unemployment results in more crime and more offenders coming before the Courts, then this in itself is likely to result in more people being in prison. Hence studies need to take account of this, and it has been found that a relationship between unemployment and imprisonment persists when variations in the level of crime have been taken into consideration (Greenberg, 1977; see also Crow *et al.*, 1989: Ch. 2, for further details).

Even so, most of the studies that have been done suffer from certain deficiencies. For example a distinction is seldom made between the different points at which employment status can have a bearing on imprisonment: at remand, at sentence, and when parole is considered. Each of these three decision points can affect not only the likelihood of imprisonment but also its duration. Furthermore, in focusing on imprisonment many studies neglect other forms of disposal. They also tend not to examine the sentencing process in any depth. In England a study was undertaken during the 1980s which aimed to address these matters. It examined sentencing at six Magistrates' Courts in different parts of the country with varying unemployment rates (Crow and Simon, 1987; Crow *et al.*, 1989: Ch. 3). The research found that unemployed offenders were significantly less likely to be fined, more likely to be given Community Service Orders, and that offenders who had a job were somewhat less likely to receive an immediate custodial sentence. With respect to custody, the differential between employed and unemployed was smaller than previous studies had led the researchers to expect, and there were no differences in the length of custodial sentence imposed. The findings in relation to use of the fine were important because use of the fine had been declining for some time, from just over 50 per cent of all offenders sentenced for indictable offences in 1978, to 39 per cent in 1986. The possibility of a link to rising unemployment had been suggested in the Criminal Statistics (Home Office, 1984a: para. 7.17), and the study provided evidence of such a link. As Figure 4.1, incorporating more recent data, demonstrates this link has persisted in recent years.

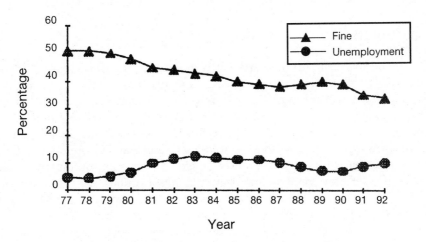

Figure 4.1   Unemployment rate (adjusted to OECD concepts) and use of the fine (for indictable offences)

Partly to overcome this vulnerability of the fine to variations in unemployment rates the Government introduced a unit fine system in the Criminal Justice Act 1991. Home Office monitoring of this legislation showed that this provision was having the desired effect of reversing the trend towards less use of the fine. In particular it was found that an increase in the use of the fine in the months following implementation of the Act was most pronounced among the unemployed (Home Office, 1993b). The Government subsequently repealed unit fines in the Criminal Justice Act 1993.

Training and jobs for offenders

Employment and reconviction

One element of any association between unemployment and crime is the extent to which offenders are likely to re-offend. In investigating employment opportunities and re-offending it is important to take account of the possibility that those offenders who do get jobs are those who would have been less likely to re-offend anyway. Allowing for this possibility, there is fairly consistent evidence that those offenders who do not have jobs are more likely to re-offend than those who do (see, for example, Farrington and Morris, 1983; Harraway *et al.*, 1985). Even allowing for such strong evidence it is important to recognise that other factors also play an important part in the likelihood of re-offending (Buickhuisen and Hoekstra, 1974).

Getting jobs

If it is the case that, (a) the harder it is to get jobs, the more likely it is that certain forms of offending will occur, and (b) those who offend and are unable to get jobs are more likely to re-offend, then the obvious corollary is to find jobs for those at risk of offending. Unfortunately this is not a simple matter, and the results of efforts to do this have not always been as clear cut as may be supposed. However, employment and training opportunities for offenders are addressed by several agencies, and it is important to consider such efforts. Employment and training opportunities may be provided by employers, by Government agencies, such as the Employment Service, by prisons, by Probation Services and by voluntary sector agencies.

It is worth noting that many offenders have found jobs of their own accord (Crow, 1979), often having more success than their professional helpers (Morris and Beverley, 1975). However, in seeking work offenders face two related problems. One is that they may have to reveal their criminal record, and the other is the likelihood that if their offending becomes known it will place them at a disadvantage in competing for jobs with non-offenders.

Studies undertaken at times of greater job availability have suggested that offenders can have a degree of success in obtaining jobs (Martin, 1962; Martin and Webster, 1971), but research has also confirmed that employers do discriminate against those with a criminal record (Boshier and Johnson, 1974). A survey of 700 employers undertaken by the Apex Trust in 1989 found that only 12 per cent of private sector respondents and 17 per cent of public sector respondents said they had knowingly employed an ex-offender in the previous year. Another barrier to employment is the fact that many offenders have little or no training. Forty-three per cent of male prisoners had no qualifications when they came into prison, compared with 34 per cent in the general male population (Walmsley *et al.*, 1992: 20). Research undertaken on schemes run by NACRO found that 70 per cent of YTS trainees had no qualifications when they joined compared with 21 per cent nationally, and 59 per cent of participants on NACRO Community Programme schemes had no qualifications compared with 25 per cent nationally (Crow *et al.*, 1989: 99, 120). Thus, despite some success in obtaining employment unaided, it is clear that most offenders need some form of assistance. This may take several forms, including having a persistent and well-informed probation officer. However, most attention tends to be directed towards a variety of schemes and projects that have come and gone over the years.

Effectiveness

An inevitable question that is asked in relation to employment and training provision for offenders is whether or not it works. This question is not easily answered for a variety of reasons. One reason is that there has been insufficient systematic evaluation of schemes. Attempts to undertake such evaluation face several difficulties. One is identifying appropriate criteria of effectiveness. One criterion is the extent to which those who have been provided with employment and training assistance re-offend. Determining this depends on a variety of considerations. For example, the primary objective of much employment and training assistance has not been specifically developed with offenders in mind and does not see addressing the circumstances and rehabilitation of offenders as its primary function. This is true of the major Government programmes. Another possible criterion is whether or not the recipients of employment and training assistance get jobs, but as mentioned already this is constrained by so many other considerations and compounded by the difficulty of ensuring that like is being compared with like.

Such studies as have been conducted have not produced a clear and decisive indication that employment and training schemes for offenders reduce offending (Crow *et al.*, 1989: 77–83). A study of the NACRO schemes during the 1980s showed that in many respects they were successful in achieving what they set out to do, by delivering good quality training to people with a background of educational and social disadvantage. Those who had been on the schemes also stood as good a chance as others on non-NACRO schemes of getting jobs subsequently, but this employment tended to be relatively short in duration. The findings also suggested that the schemes 'contained' offending while people were taking part in them, but follow-up showed that offending rose once people left the schemes (Crow *et al.*, 1989). Like other areas of work with offenders, employment and training schemes have been affected by the 'nothing works' ethos that has prevailed since the mid-1970s. This is unfortunate because not only could it be argued that employment is a rather different phenomenon to the kind of treatment regimes that gave rise to the 'nothing works' conclusions, but those conclusions have in any case come under critical scrutiny (Gendreau and Ross, 1979; Raynor and Vanstone, 1993). Schemes are not themselves 'real' jobs, they are limited in length and scope and income, and a shortage of real job opportunities means that offenders often simply do not have the opportunity to get the jobs that might prevent re-offending. It is arguable therefore that the case for the effectiveness of employment schemes as a means of rehabilitation is not proven. The indications are that employment and training schemes for offenders do have an important role to play, but cannot themselves alter the overall job situation. This is supported by consistent evidence that offenders who do get jobs are less likely to re-offend. This leads to the conclusion that it is the overall level of unemployment that is crucial, and that what is needed is a sufficient supply of jobs of the kind that offenders and potential offenders would have access to. This does not mean that employment and training provision for offenders is of no value. Indeed, quite the reverse: it suggests that more provision is needed in order that careful investigation can be undertaken to find out and ensure that the most suitable and effective opportunities are available. What we know so far suggests:

- that it is necessary to have what used to be termed 'special needs' provision which takes account of the background and capability of the large majority of people who are most at risk of offending;
- that adequate income is important, so that there is an incentive to participate in worthwhile training and work rather than on illicit means of income generation; and
- that schemes need to have real prospects of leading to employment.

Editors' commentary

As this chapter has exemplified, simple conclusions about the nature of the relationship between unemployment and offending are to be avoided. The author outlines the need to consider both the nature of unemployment – issues of length and future prospects – and those factors which impinge on employment and crime levels such as poverty, social deprivation, drug use and changes in law enforcement policy. In other words, we cannot claim a direct causal link between unemployment and crime. Most practitioners, however, would find it difficult to disagree with the proposition that finding a job is a major step on the path to a lifestyle that is free of offending. Indeed the studies highlighted in this chapter show that unemployment is a factor which has impact on crime levels (albeit within the context of a range of other economic factors); that mass unemployment and increased crime levels are linked; that the link between the two is of particular significance for young people (being young and unemployed heightens the risk of offending); that there is a lack of a focus on women; and that there is a higher proportion of unemployment among black people.

We therefore agree with the core of the argument in the chapter, that the extent of unemployment among people who find themselves on the caseloads of probation officers makes it imperative that a well thought out and coherent strategy for addressing the problem is a key feature of probation practice. It can be argued that to some degree it has always been a component of practice, and that increasingly Probation Services are ensuring that it is (James and Bottomley, 1994). However, we contend that it is often taking place at an individual level with the concomitant problems of isolation and lack of support.

Broad (1991) provides a useful elucidation of the problems facing the Probation Service in the area of employment. Although his is an examination of just one team's approach to a community orientation to probation, the dearth of descriptions of employment focused work in the literature suggests that the picture painted is not untypical. While acknowledging the degree of effort invested by the team in increasing the employment prospects of individuals, Broad argues that the failure to address unemployment as a social issue meant that,

> The opportunity to present the team's 'employment work' within a broader social justice framework (necessarily but very problematically concerned amongst other things, with addressing structural, financial and resource inequalities) were denied and avoided – essentially beyond reach. (1991: 114)

Among other things, he found that in social inquiry reports there was a virtual absence of any attempt to describe a link between the high local and national unemployment, and as a consequence the problem of unemployment was 'individualised rather than contextualised'.

In effect, Broad exposes the limitations of the traditional probation approach to the problem devoid as it can be of any broader strategic considerations. In accepting his analysis, like him, we do not deny the value of probation activity premised on the notion of increasing individual employment prospects. At its most basic, this involves direct contact with employers and developing a network of patronage – activity that fitted more comfortably in the days of relatively low unemployment. The social skills and problem-solving approach (Priestley *et al.*, 1978) inaugurated more sophisticated skills-based work involving reassessment of marketable skills, application form filling, the refinement of telephone and interview skills, and the shaping of job search strategies. Its impact on practice is easily underestimated, and although this type of work has been superseded by the general availability of job clubs and training provision, it still influences the work undertaken with clients in individual face-to-face work.

In a recent study of standard probation practice by one of the editors (Vanstone, 1994), an analysis of probation officers' records revealed that a significant amount of face-to-face work with probationers was taken up with attempts to help with a range of practical problems, prominent among which was unemployment. However, more time was spent on this specific area with men than with women, a point taken up later in this Commentary.

There is, therefore, much that an individual probation officer can still do, and this might include ensuring that the plight of individuals is placed firmly within the context of levels of unemployment and restricted opportunity. However, it is only at the level of the organisation that attempts to have impact on its structural dimension can be made and these need to include campaigning by individual Chief Probation Officers within their local sphere of influence. Of equal importance is the need for the National Association of Probation Officers and the Association of Chief Probation Officers at a national level to plead the special case of unemployed probation clients and, among them, those who face duplicate problems because they are also black, gay or disabled. Local Services and the national organisations can have significant impact in terms of enhancing the profile of the problem through basic monitoring of, for instance, the degree to which previous convictions and racial discrimination can affect employment prospects. Another major contribution can come from more ambitious sponsoring of research, of which the ACOP and NAPO sponsored research on the financial circumstances of young offenders is an excellent example (Stewart and Stewart, 1993a: Ch. 4).

The context of employment training is important and during the 1970s and 1980s Government agencies have developed such provision, from the Youth Opportunities Programme to Employment Training and Training for Work. The trend has been towards a greater emphasis on training, and, as a result of the growing management role of the Training Enterprise Councils (TECs), tighter structures. It could be argued that this tightening up of structures coupled with increased pressure to produce successful training outcomes has disadvantaged people who offend because they are riskier bets. Whatever the truth of this is, it is critically important for Probation Services to link with TECs and other prime movers in the field such as the APEX Trust and NACRO.

An interesting example of the outcome of such collaboration is *Prisoners Into Jobs*, a guide for staff in the Prison and Probation Services produced in the late 1980s by the Training Agency, APEX, NACRO, the Employment Service, the Prison Service and ACOP. It covers a number of specific areas which include keeping prisoners' jobs open; dealing with the problem of previous convictions; getting prisoners into training; self-employment; and responding to the particular needs of women and black women and men (Training Agency, 1989). More recently APEX has produced recommendations for productive partnerships between the TECs, the Prison Service and the Probation Service, in which it highlights (as a model) the way the Lancashire Probation Service provides funding for outreach work in prisons by education and employment coordinators (APEX Trust, 1993).

As we have indicated, there are clear limits on what individual officers can achieve in this area of work, and it is, therefore, vitally important for probation boards and managements to pay more than lip service; pious words in glossy annual reports are not enough. ACOP has produced valuable advice to areas in this respect (ACOP, 1989) and its guidelines for practice are well worth revisiting. They suggest a broad strategy which includes the production of an area policy with clear objectives; this includes advice to officers to discuss employment with all people on their caseloads, and to address the issue in all reports. It also promotes liaison and networking with local employers and all other relevant bodies, the establishing of local offender employment forums (with union representation) to promote the needs of offenders and the seeking of places on the TECs. An equal emphasis is placed on the monitoring of the effectiveness of policies, the need to understand the economic developments in the area, the appointment of specialist staff (as for instance, in the Employment unit of South Glamorgan Probation Service), active lobbying of relevant bodies, and promoting training events and conferences on the issue. This seems to us to contain all the major ingredients required for a Service to begin a genuine process of impacting on the structural dimensions of the problem.

In South Glamorgan the Service appointed a specialist employment worker in 1991 with the result that a number of initiatives have been established. They include a Forum on offender employment which brings together all relevant agencies and organisations. Its activities include providing specific advice on the employment problems of probation clients, developing employer partnerships and encouraging positive publicity about success. Linked to this is the Future Skills project (jointly funded by British Gas, South Wales Electricity, South Glamorgan County Council, the TEC and probation and European social funds) which endeavours to secure training and education provision for probation clients.

An equally interesting example of a Probation Service promoting a broad strategy as recommended by ACOP can be seen in the work emerging from the Community Development Unit in Cleveland (Cleveland Probation Service, 1993). Under the overall direction of a community development officer (employment), the Service has established an employment service adviser in four of the offices whose role is to channel clients to mainstream and specialist provision in training and employment; provide follow up support; match clients to job vacancies, and liaise with supervising probation officers. In addition it has set up the Hope Project which incorporates the use of volunteers trained to assist clients in job search; employment link officers in each team; a regular information exchange, and a community development officer operating in an advisory capacity. Significantly, some of the work such as the Job Ready Club which specifically helps those people who are not ready to gain access to mainstream services, is premised on the principle of partnership and funded by a combination of sources including Safer Cities.

Coordinated and well supported initiatives like those in South Glamorgan and Cleveland create more potential for addressing the particular problems of disadvantaged people. Women and black offenders are two groups facing a double jeopardy – unemployment coupled with gender and race. Dominelli and McLeod (1989) in their critique of social work practice in the area of women and unemployment, provide a template for action which is easily transferable to work with female offenders. They enunciate a persuasive argument that (ironically during the era of the first woman Prime Minister) women have been increasingly pressed either back into the home or into lowly paid non-unionised jobs. The effect of this has been that now the majority of women who come into contact with social services provision are either without paid employment, or in low-paid jobs and caring for dependants, or without paid employment and in positions of dependency because of infirmity or old age. Like female probation clients, they will also be living in poverty. Moreover, their problems will be exacerbated by the fact that practice is often permeated by the acceptance of the status quo ('women manage'), and also concentrates on welfare rights to the exclusion of other concerns.

We believe that Dominelli and McLeod's proposals for action in wider social work are applicable to probation work, and enhance the quality of provision to what is often a marginalised group. They advocate an action strategy in which social workers routinely raise the issue of training and career opportunities with women, provide advice and information, and create self-help groups (see Jones *et al.*, 1991, for an interesting probation example). In addition they argue the need for union activity on behalf of women, and the provision of counselling support which focuses specifically on the problems facing women who re-enter training, further education and employment. An essential corollary to these, they suggest, is work with male partners to deal with attitudes which inhibit and constrain women's efforts to do so. Finally, they stress the importance of forming networks with women's employment projects, and campaigning more widely on relevant issues. It may be particularly important for female probation clients to be linked with feminist networks, and in order for such a strategy to stand any chance of success within the Probation Service, it would need to be supported and owned by management.

An interesting practice example of such a strategy is the Women Offenders' Outreach Project (WOOPS) created by Nottinghamshire Probation Service in 1993. This focuses on the particular problems faced by women, offers employment-related guidance and counselling, and attempts to mobilise resources and opportunities on their behalf. Particular attention is paid to issues for women who are in transition from working in the home to further training, education and employment.

We know, also, that finding employment is severely hampered by racism which is a structural problem in itself. Denny (1992) in a description of a hypothetical probation team intent on initiating a project designed to assist probation clients deal with racism in employment, suggests that it would enable black probationers and probation officers 'to explore jointly the ramifications and manifestations of racism in this crucial area of everyday life and may connect with the developments of strategies for finding work' (1992: 153). This would avoid the potential problem of individually focused work ignoring the wider structural problems. Denny cites the Handsworth alternative scheme, a probation linked project which specifically liaises with training and employment projects run by black people, as a model to follow. It seems to us that the kind of forum created by the Black Offender Initiative in Inner London (Jenkins and Lawrence, 1992) gives a voice to the employment concerns and problems of black probationers, and could be used specifically to influence the policy and practice of the agency.

A helpful focus on the final area with which we deal in this Commentary – self-employment – is provided by Rieple and Harper (1993) in their study of the provision of training for ex-offenders in small business or self-employment skills. While they have found no evidence that ex-offenders have entrepreneurial attitudes above the normal population, they have found that a significant number have either been in their own business, or intend to do so. They present convincing arguments for the Probation Service treating them as a special group; in particular, the fact that they are likely to experience greater than normal problems in relation to financial capital and credit facilities. Encouragingly, although their survey indicates a high degree of ignorance among probation officers about self-employment possibilities, they have found an increasing number of services employing in-house specialists, and building relationships with APEX, NACRO and organisations such as the Prince's Youth Business Trust.

Although it is unwise to oversimplify the link between unemployment and crime, securing a job is likely to be a significant step towards an offence-free lifestyle. The Probation Service, in conjunction with other bodies, can help people to take that step; its capacity to do so is, however, dependent on a commitment to coherent policies and properly resourced strategies.

5 Housing

Gill Stewart

Housing is where we live and as such it provides the most immediate social context for individual behaviour. Housing is home – be it a hostel, a high-rise flat, a van or a mansion – and home and its contents are as significant to personal identity as are the clothes we wear (Dittmar, 1992). Yet in this country at this time, we have ultimately no right to be housed; there are, for instance, rights to evict and to limited short-term protection from eviction, but no right of access for people without any home. Attitudes behind the policies are indicated by language: in many contexts 'housing' is synonymous with 'property' and the two words are used interchangeably, denoting something to be acquired or inherited, an investment as much as a dwelling place.

Policies and systems

The national housing stock is notionally divided into sectors according to ownership, the main ones being owner-occupied, public rented and private rented. According to Government statistics, two-thirds of households are owner-occupiers most of whom are repaying a loan which is usually a building society mortgage. Compared with other European countries, the owner-occupied sector in England is much larger and generally more expensive, the private rented sector is smaller, and the public sector more residual; these differences are less marked in the rest of the UK. Housing conditions are worst in the two rented sectors, where there are disproportionate concentrations of people who are young and single, old or disabled, unemployed, black, lone parents. A third of new tenants moving into the public sector have previously been homeless (Central Statistical Office, 1994; Stewart and Stewart, 1993b).

Distinguished as they are mainly by formal legal ownership, the housing sectors do not constitute an integral system from the point of view of practitioners and service users who are trying to gain access. 'Systems' are characterised as a functional whole with interrelated parts; they may appear impenetrable and protectionist but, with skill and experience, can be 'worked' to the user's advantage. The National Health Service and the social security scheme are prominent examples. Public sector housing does have many of the features of a system, although with significant local variations, but there are few points of connection with the private sectors.

It is hard to discern a national housing policy, beyond the ideological promotion of private ownership and consequent attempts to dismantle the public sector by selling council houses and cutting expenditure more drastically than in any other area of the welfare state. As a result, new building by local authorities in the 1990s stands at less than 10 per cent of the annual rate during the 1960s, while there are ever increasing numbers of homeless people.

Among the diverse policies which have an impact on housing costs, availability and security, the emphasis has been restrictive and repressive. Thus the first half of 1994 saw Treasury proposals for extensive rent rises combined with further cuts in housing benefit; more reductions in the mortgage interest payable through income support; and tighter criteria aimed at reducing 'severe hardship' payments to disqualified under-18 year olds. Significant erosions of rights for homeless people were planned (Department of the Environment, 1994); squatting and the travelling lifestyle were being criminalised in a Criminal Justice and Public Order Bill; and yet another attempt was made to close board and lodging 'dole hostels' through changes in planning regulations.

This list makes depressing but familiar reading for probation officers; it also illustrates complexity in the range of policies which potentially affect clients' housing circumstances, and their interaction with major policy systems for social security and criminal justice. That complexity may make it difficult for practitioners to intervene over individuals' housing problems. Yet probation officers can develop familiarity with, and expertise in, local systems which most affect their clients and thereby become effective in achieving change. It was a city probation team which uncovered an earlier attempt to close board and lodging hotels and criminalise their residents using social security powers of fraud investigation. Probation support led to many claimants being acquitted or released without charge, and achieved national publicity for the broader issues (Franey, 1986; Stewart *et al.*, 1986).

Probation clients' circumstances

There is substantial research evidence to show that offenders under Probation Service supervision are disadvantaged in housing terms compared with the general population (as described above) and also with the clientele of other major agencies. Very few probation clients are owner-occupiers: practically none were found in nationally representative caseload surveys conducted for the Association of Chief Officers of Probation (ACOP) and the National Association of Probation Officers (NAPO). Only the Home Office's survey of prisoners found more than one in ten to have been home owners before imprisonment, but a third of them had to sell while in custody (Stewart and Stewart, 1991; Walmsley *et al.*, 1992; NAPO, 1993).

Compatible surveys of Probation Service clients, and those of Social Services Departments and Citizens' Advice Bureaux, showed that probation clients are less likely to have secure council tenancies and more likely to be living in private lodgings or bed and breakfast, hostels or with relatives (Stewart and Stewart, 1991: 17). The ACOP study of under-25 year olds under statutory supervision found that nearly half had no independent accommodation but were staying with parents or in someone else's house-hold, mostly on a temporary basis. In all three surveys noted above one in twenty offenders were found to be literally homeless; more among those who were on remand, before probation officers had started to work with them. The incidence of homelessness was the same in the mid-1960s (Davies, 1969: 26).

The material disadvantage of offenders under supervision, in terms of their income and employment, as well as housing, and their reliance on state benefits and services, has led some commentators (e.g. Jordan and Jones, 1988) to present them as part of an 'underclass' or a 'dependency culture'. That is one way of analysing the social context of 'offending behaviour' but, in common with other deviancy subculture theories, the concept of under-class is both theoretically problematic and potentially stigmatising (Dean and Taylor Gooby, 1992). A more satisfactory explanation can be derived from mainstream control theory, whereby the ability and motivation of relevant social institutions (family, schools) to influence young people's behaviour breaks down under conditions of structural inequality and oppressive social policies (this argument is developed in Stewart *et al.*, 1994).

Theoretical explanations are, by their very nature, concerned with wide social groups at a level of generality. For an understanding of individual circumstances and the requirements of practice, we must return to agency-based research. While acknowledging the significance of relative housing deprivation as a background factor for probation work in general, we need to know the extent to which housing features among the specific problems which are presented to practitioners, and the origins of individual housing problems.

In the ACOP study, probation officers were currently working on housing issues in a third of the cases, which was considerably less than employment but more than poverty and financial problems (Pearson, 1989, highlights the continued expectation of finding work and dominance of the 'rehabilitative ideal' in probation work, despite mass unemployment). Similar findings are further evidenced in the ACOP, NAPO and Home Office surveys, and see the chapters in this book by Crow (Chapter 4) and Arnold and Jordan (Chapter 3). Material issues generally were regarded as being among the most pressing problems presented by offenders under supervision and in many cases their urgency precluded any other consideration. In contrast, only one in thirteen people on community service orders (CSO) reported housing problems in McIvor's (1991) study; but having unsettled accommodation was also a reason for offenders being considered unsuitable for a CSO, so most in that position had already been screened out at sentencing stage.

Research evidence about offenders' housing problems is sparse, especially considering the importance of the issue, but looking back at past studies, we discover that their findings are remarkably consistent with the ACOP work cited above. In the mid-1960s a third of probationers were assessed by researchers as having 'material stress' in their living conditions (Davies, 1969). In the early 1970s one-third, again, of probationers in the IMPACT experiment were living in hostels or lodgings or were literally homeless. That finding was based on self-assessment, and respondents rated their housing problems most seriously (Folkard *et al.*, 1976). Returning to the 1990s, one in eight inmates in the Walmsley national prison survey said that more help with finding accommodation would be the most useful service that could be provided to prepare them for release; only money and home leave were rated higher. Overall two conclusions emerge from the evidence: that a third of offenders under probation supervision have problems with housing, and that such problems are very important to those who experience them.

Information about the nature and origins of offenders' housing problems is available from the same range of research sources. Locating the origins of people's housing problems in their personal circumstances does not imply that the issue is individualised and therefore fragmented. Someone may need to find different accommodation because of, for instance, the family situation; but it is the shortage of available and affordable housing which then renders him or her homeless. The housing system, in its broadest sense, is the root cause of housing problems rather than individual behaviour which, in this area, is properly viewed within a structural and policy context. By looking at personal circumstances, we can understand the pressures which leave people vulnerable to the inadequacies of the system.

Similar arguments apply to poverty, which is a major constraint on housing opportunity: low income and lack of capital inhibit access to the 'property market', so owner-occupation or better quality private renting are out of the question for most probation clients, only a fifth of whom are in waged employment and two-thirds of whom have weekly benefit incomes of under £40 for themselves and any dependants. But the process which turns this context of routine poverty into immediate financial crises for individuals, is linked to what is going on in their personal lives. The evidence for this comes from research into use of the Social Fund where three-quarters of probation clients (a much higher proportion than in other agencies) were known recently to have experienced a stressful 'life event' which strained their financial resources to the limit of coping. Those 'life events' included leaving home, incarceration, relationship breakdown, and the birth or death of a close relative (Stewart *et al.*, 1989; Stewart and Stewart, 1991).

Looking now at the circumstances which turn the general context of housing disadvantage into housing problems for individuals, we find a similar range of events in their personal lives. One of the most consistent findings of research into offenders' backgrounds is a lack of stability in their family and personal relationships. In the ACOP study, probation officers reported that family issues had been significant in the onset of offending for two-thirds of clients, notably lack of support or guidance, and rejection, poor relations with a step parent; and parental abuse or neglect.

Leaving home and finding independent accommodation is an important transition for young people entering adulthood, and it is the point at which they have their first direct encounter with the housing 'system'. Offenders under supervision are likely to have left home earlier than average for their age group and social class (16 being the peak age for leaving), and for overwhelmingly negative reasons associated with family conflict. One in four are known to have been in care during their childhood, a finding which is consistent between the ACOP research, the Home Office's national prison survey and local studies in Nottinghamshire and the south west (Nottinghamshire Probation Service, 1990: 10; Pritchard *et al.*, 1992). For young people who were brought up in care or who left home in a state of conflict, being unable to rely on family support when things go wrong puts them at increased risk of homelessness.

Another major constraint on opportunity is public sector housing policies which discriminate, for example in favour of families with children and therefore against single people.

As leaving care is a housing pressure point, so too is leaving custody. Half of the respondents in the national prisoners' survey who were near their release date did not expect to return to where they had been living before imprisonment. Even when no change of accommodation is planned, other factors may cast doubt on the viability of existing arrangements. Accumulated debts can threaten the security of a tenancy which is still formally available to a discharged prisoner, and family relations may have worsened under the strain of imprisonment to a point where living together proves to be no longer possible (Paylor, 1992).

Half of prisoners' marriages do not survive a five-year sentence and one in ten split up within six months of imprisonment; it seems probable that many more relationships deteriorate and end some time after release. Relationship breakdown commonly means that both partners have to find somewhere else to live. Initially men tend to move back to their mothers or another relative, then into lodgings or a hostel while, especially if there has been violence, this is the stage at which women with children are likely to become homeless prior to getting a council tenancy of their own. Even if they have never been in custody, offenders under supervision appear to experience relationship breakdown younger and more frequently than average (for example a third of 23 year olds in the ACOP study had already been through at least one marriage type of relationship).

The combination of unreliable family support, institutional experience and unstable relationships can make Probation Service clients unusually liable to housing problems which they lack the personal and material resources to solve on their own. The consequences are dependence on relatives who may be in no better position themselves; and having to live in poor quality, temporary, unhealthy and often relatively high cost housing financed (inadequately) from housing benefit. The implications for individuals can be feelings of insecurity and powerlessness, and lack of privacy or independence. Homelessness in particular is all-absorbing, and an unsafe and damaging living environment is a major source of instability. We know that clients' housing problems are very important to them and that probation officers' help with housing problems is highly valued.

Housing and crime

The question 'Does housing disadvantage cause crime?' is even more problematic than 'Do poverty or unemployment cause crime?'

There is a common difficulty with establishing causal relationships while avoiding crude determinism. Macro statistical connections have been made between economic recession, youth unemployment, levels of imprisonment and national rates of recorded crime (for example in Dickinson, 1994); but nothing at a comparably large scale has been attempted on housing and crime, perhaps because the issue lacks the political immediacy of unemployment.

What recent evidence we do have about housing and crime comes mainly from research undertaken during the past decade on victimisation and situational crime prevention (e.g. successive British Crime Surveys, and Hope and Shaw, 1988). This indicates that property crime, especially domestic burglary and vandalism, is concentrated on the poorest council estates which are regarded by housing managers as 'difficult to let'. The concentration is particularly marked in England, where the public and private sectors are most polarised.

Compare that evidence on the spatial distribution of crime with what we already know about the housing circumstances of offenders under supervision. While the ACOP survey found that only a fifth of Probation Service clients had their own council tenancy, a much larger group (three-fifths) were staying with their parents or other relatives on council estates, meaning that around three-quarters overall were living in public sector housing. Many were from those same poorer, unpopular estates where so much crime occurs.

Putting those two sets of research information together it would appear, circumstantially, that many of the people whose 'offending behaviour' results in their appearing in court and being put under probation supervision tend to live in places where there is also a high risk of becoming the victim of certain types of crime: the housing contexts are broadly similar. It would be logical to conclude that, in those circumstances, offenders are themselves also likely to be victims, and this impression is confirmed in an exploratory study of probationers' experiences of being victimised (Peelo *et al.*, 1992).

In some respects, offending in high crime areas may be perceived as conformity to a social norm, whereby a certain type and level of criminal activity is condoned within the family and the broader community. The criminal justice system also plays a key role, in keeping the residents of so-called 'problem estates' under exceptional public scrutiny while neglecting their status as victims and criminalising what are essentially coping strategies in the face of poverty, such as benefit or fuel meter fraud and avoiding the television licence fee.

Women with children and in multiple debt are especially vulnerable to that process of criminalisation. The other group most likely to be involved in survival offending is homeless 16 and 17 year olds who are disqualified because of their age from claiming benefits (this analysis of offending behaviour is extended and developed in Stewart *et al.*, 1994). Having 'no fixed address' to give in Court also carries an increased likelihood of remand in custody: both the ACOP and Home Office surveys found the level of homelessness among unconvicted remand prisoners, at 25 per cent, to be twice that of the prison population overall. It thus seems that the criminal justice system makes an essentially punitive response to homelessness, as Box (1987) has shown that it does to unemployment.

I have already argued that imprisonment tends to worsen people's housing circumstances on release. There is also evidence to suggest that imprisonment brings an increased risk of offenders' homes being burgled when they are inside and their personal possessions 'lost' at the point of reception into custody or stolen by relatives and friends with whom they have been left for safe keeping, while high levels of theft are reported by residents of bail and probation hostels. The criminal justice system appears to leave offenders who are in its own accommodation unusually open to victimisation (Peelo *et al.*, 1992).

In conclusion, certain housing circumstances make both offending and being victimised more likely, and the criminal justice system tends to amplify that likelihood and also to worsen offenders' housing options. A complex process of interaction is apparent between the housing contexts of committing and 'receiving' crime and the operation of the criminal justice system.

Responding to housing issues in probation work

The baseline implications for probation work of housing issues, as I have outlined them, are that not engaging with them means neglecting an offender's most immediate social context, which risks hindering whatever else the worker and client are trying to do. These conclusions are reached, by different routes, in both academic research and Home Office policy documents. Practical, material crises in general and homelessness in particular tend to monopolise time and distract attention from other issues. Unresolved they may result in a lessening of confidence in the probation officer and consequent difficulty in achieving the objectives of supervision which, at their most basic, include reporting and not re-offending.

For instance the Home Office's 1988 Green Paper, on the subject of additional requirements attached to orders, recognised that 'living in poor or isolated accommodation' could make a condition unenforceable (para. 3.18). In the original *National Standards*, a housing crisis would be an obvious example of 'chaotic lifestyle or substantial difficulties' which could acceptably explain failure to comply with a probation order, thus absolving the probation officer of a duty to report breach (Home Office, 1992: para. 3.3.25).

Housing problems have long been regarded as difficult and therefore unpopular with probation officers and local authority social workers alike. Influential Home Office research by Davies in the 1960s found that probation officers were least likely to form and sustain a 'casework relationship' with those clients who were under the greatest 'environmental stress', and that:

> Even when probation officers spent much effort in relation to accommodation problems this was rarely successful. [It was unclear] whether this was due to the intractable nature of the problems, to inappropriate treatment, or to lack of relevant resources ... It can be concluded that the probation officers played virtually no part in the active amelioration of their clients' living conditions. The service simply did not have the time, or did not think it a part of its duty, to do anything about improving the home circumstances in a material sense. In almost all cases where material conditions were felt to be critical, the onus for bringing about an improvement was left with the client. (Davies, 1969: 109, 121; Davies, 1974: 58, 60)

Home Office IMPACT researchers in the 1970s described the level of help given for accommodation and material problems generally as 'surprisingly low'. A third of the probationers allocated to specially reduced caseloads were living in hostels or were literally homeless, but probation officers gave help with finding better housing to less than a tenth. While this finding alone did not account for the unsuccessful outcome of the whole IMPACT experiment, neither can it have helped.

A further study by Davies in the late 1980s found that probation officers were by then much more active in relation to housing issues than the researchers had expected, particularly in field teams, throughcare and day centres (Boswell *et al.*, 1993). In the early 1990s, the ACOP research reported that probation officers were working on clients' housing problems in a third of cases and that this level of involvement was consistent around the country, indicating that it was a well established aspect of practice. In contrast, wide local variations were found in welfare rights activity by probation officers, to do with poverty and financial problems.

Evidently housing issues are well on the way to becoming a central concern for practitioners in today's Probation Service. This is happening at a particularly unpropitious time when political pressures and managerial priorities have been moving towards an increasingly narrow view of core tasks evolving around 'tackling offending behaviour', with other activities marginalised or contracted out. Following from the Audit Commission's prescription of the supervising officer as an overseeing 'case manager', the 1990 Green Paper declared that: 'Arranging for, and actually providing accommodation for offenders are both functions which require expertise distinct from professional probation skills', and should appropriately be done by the voluntary or private sectors. That voluntary housing agencies are happy to go along with this policy was seen in their evidence to the Prison Service Inspectorate's review of throughcare (Chief Inspector of Prisons, 1985).

Probation workers generally seem to be moving beyond or around the officially de-contextualised view of 'offending behaviour' and increasingly addressing their clients' social circumstances, working from within the new managerialist culture, which is a 'remarkable' achievement, to slightly misquote Graham Smith, the Chief Inspector of Probation (1993). In the rest of this chapter I shall discuss some important points relating to housing that arise from this work at individual, administrative, interagency and struc-tural levels.

Individual structural levels

Awareness of the housing context is a prerequisite for improving practice in direct work with clients. Practitioners need to 'think housing' when making an initial assessment and planning the programme of supervision. In through-care work, prisoners' housing prospects on release from custody should be anticipated and any arrangements made in advance. Problematic housing circumstances and their implications should be explained in pre-sentence and pre-discharge reports. Probation workers need to remain open to recognising common issues arising from recurring individual circumstances, and act on these at other levels, as outlined below.

NAPO made a valuable contribution to improving housing awareness by establishing a housing working party in the mid-1980s and publishing a resource pack for members which was launched with an exhortation: 'We confidently assert that the provision of decent housing generates [positive] attitudes and that it is important to develop such opportunities for clients' (NAPO, 1985). However, changing attitudes among professional workers can be a long process and, as with racism and sexism, stigmatising language constitutes a barrier to more positive ways of thinking and relating to people. For instance, negative stereotyping of homeless offenders as 'NFAs' (meaning people with 'no fixed address') has contributed to the provision of a second class Probation Service for this group, who are already disadvantaged by the social security system and housing policies. Talk of 'problem families' who inhabit 'problem estates' is another example. There is a need to bring housing and poverty issues generally within the fold of anti-discriminatory practice. The dimension has been notably absent from debates about discrimination and equal opportunities, just as social class has gone missing from the accepted list of social divisions headed by race and gender. There is no mention of housing, poverty or social class in the relevant sections of *National Standards* (Home Office, 1995c).

Administrative structural levels

As the Probation Service is organised on a geographical basis, with field teams being responsible for clients referred from local catchment populations, administrative matters, such as where the office is situated, can have implications for the important questions of accessibility and accountability to the community. These concerns were addressed by areas, including Nottinghamshire and Merseyside, which reorganised on neighbourhood or 'patch' principles (Henderson, 1987), but it took high-profile 'riots' to bring such issues to the attention of a wider audience within the probation service. Reports about disturbances in Brixton, Inner London, and on the Meadowell housing estate in Northumbria concluded that the probation teams had become too geographically remote from, and out of touch with, their local communities (Broad, 1991; North *et al.*, 1992). The recommended solution was to move back among the people, to have at least a reporting office in the neighbourhood where most clients live.

There are pros and cons, however, to greater community integration. One consequence may be increased distance and alienation from the professional mainstream, as was experienced by the social work team based on the Broadwater Farm housing estate in north east London after the 'riots' there (Hutchinson-Reis, 1986). Two decades ago Davies (1974) were warning probation officers of the risks attached to over-identification with a deviant client group; that vulnerability can be amplified when the population concerned is also exceptionally disadvantaged.

Whether the Service should have housing specialists, or teams working exclusively with homeless offenders, is another organisational issue with pros and cons. On the pro side, the clients of such specialists probably get a service which is more responsive to their circumstances and their particular needs. An argument against is that the existence of specialists reinforces the political view, which I have already mentioned, that housing is not a core task in mainstream probation work, and workers in field teams may be encouraged to abdicate responsibility for their clients' housing problems by referring on to the specialists. In response to this dilemma, some Homeless Offender Units, most of which were previously called After-Care Units, have been renamed Housing Teams. They now deal with the housing needs of a broader clientele than homeless discharged prisoners, also acting as an advisory resource to colleagues rather than necessarily taking over supervision.

Systems and structures

Looking now beyond the internal organisation of the area Probation Service, systems intervention involves working with other agencies in the locality. Probation officers generally are very much aware of the value of local contacts: knowledge about local resources is rated second in importance only to sentencing principles as a requirement for practice, and hostels and landladies are given as prominent examples (Boswell *et al.*, 1993). The Home Office circular about Area Accommodation Strategies (1988b) represented a central attempt to introduce principles of economic efficiency and to standardise a diversity of often semi-informal contact systems which already existed at local levels. An initiative such as this could prompt the development of a more coherent range of 'offender housing', but might equally prove counterproductive by insisting on enforced 'partnerships between agencies with very different status and priorities (as argued by Day, 1988).

Interagency work can be time-consuming, requiring delicate negotiation within an unequal power balance. Research on probation involvement in multi-agency projects on 'difficult' housing estates suggests that police representatives tend to dominate the agenda to the detriment of probation concerns (Blagg *et al.* in Hope and Shaw, 1988). Situational crime prevention is likely to be a police priority on a high-crime estate and while that can make a significant difference to victimisation patterns, its impact on overall levels of offending may be only superficial when the social context of lack of opportunity and environmental neglect remain untouched.

The case has been made (in Raynor *et al.*, 1994) for probation commitment to social crime prevention which moves beyond intervention in existing agency systems, with their shortcomings and limitations, to concentrate on improving the social infrastructure in areas of housing disadvantage: more leisure facilities for young people, better public transport and utilities, support networks for lone parents, protection for vulnerable minorities. That structural approach is consistent with a way of understanding 'offending behaviour' which focuses on social circumstances rather than isolated criminal acts.

Conclusion

In this chapter I have reviewed evidence about the housing circumstances of probation clients, raised issues around the links between housing and crime, and discussed the nature of responses to housing disadvantage in probation practice. It remains for me to suggest how improved performance in this area could assist the Probation Service in tackling offending. The main point is that awareness of, and engagement with, housing problems can make the experience of probation supervision more relevant to clients' lives, thus enhancing the prospect of behavioural change. When 'offending behaviour' and criminal acts are addressed within their social context, it becomes harder for clients to disown them.

An improvement in the quality of information about offenders' social circumstances made available to the Court should contribute to more appropriate sentencing and reduce the likelihood of criminalisation for survival offending (a diversion scheme with the criminal justice system for homeless first offenders could be even more effective). A probation commitment to social crime prevention would enhance opportunities and offer some positive choices to people who live in the most deprived parts of the community and who, in many senses, are also victims themselves. Housing presents some difficult challenges to probation workers but when they respond the rewards are worthwhile.

Editors' commentary

This Commentary begins with an irony. Of all the subjects covered in this volume accommodation is probably the area where – unevenly and sporadically – most progress can be identified in the development of a systems approach within the Probation Service. It is also the sphere of core social service provision which has suffered the greatest cutbacks during the Conservative years since 1979. The collapse of public provision was so dramatic that between 1976/7 and 1988/9 expenditure on housing fell from 4.1 per cent to 1.6 per cent of gross domestic product (Lowe, 1993).

An explanation of this perverse phenomenon lies beyond the scope of this book but factors include both the tangible nature of the issue – here is a problem where the results of effort are directly visible – and the new prominence of Housing Associations in Government channelling of funds for particular housing needs. In this section we will attempt to show how, at a variety of different levels, action has been possible to address this most basic social issue in a way which is beyond the offending of individuals. These levels include the Governmental, the Service level, cooperation with other agencies and the initiative of groups of workers.

Of these levels the Governmental remains the most ambivalent. As Gill Stewart makes plain, the initiatives which Government has taken in respect of particular groups with accommodation needs has to be set against the general, and more powerful, set of actions which it has taken in cutting expenditure in this area and favouring private as against public forms of ownership and tenure. Time and again local Services, in reporting their efforts to improve accommodation prospects for users in their areas, emphasise the lengthening waiting lists and diminution of local authority housing stock, as the background against which these efforts have to be made. The prison building programme has, of course, been the single greatest beneficiary of Conservative policies in the law and order field. Outside that protected core developments have been dominated by the varying climate of public expenditure, producing a policy see-saw in which the plans of today are the waste paper of tomorrow. Hostel places are the single most prominent example of these changes. In February 1992 the then Home Secretary, Kenneth Baker, announced that an extra 800 bail beds were to be created over the next three years. £26 million were put aside for the capital works needed to support these plans, with an additional £4–5 million in revenue. Two years later the process was sent into complete reverse. On 4 April 1994, the Home Office ordered shutting of 11 bail hostels, losing 270 places, a cut overall of 10 per cent.

Such decisions, of course, have a direct impact upon the demand for offender accommodation in other parts of the criminal justice system. In the 12 months to April 1994 the remand population in prisons in England and Wales rose by 30 per cent. At the same time the NACRO report *Prison Overcrowding – Recent Developments* recorded the:

> sharp rise in the prison population which has taken place during 1993 and so far in 1994. At the end of February 1994 the prison population was 5024 higher than 12 months earlier (47,906 compared to 42,882). During that time the overall prison population increased by 12%, an average increase of 419 a month, while the number of prisoners on remand rose by 20%.
>
> To cope with numbers increasing at this rate, the Prison Service would need to open a prison the size of Dartmoor every six weeks. (NACRO, 1994)

Hostel places were an essential part of the second strand in this review of accommodation strategies – the local Service Plan. In 1988 the Home Office issued Circular 35/1988 which placed upon local Services an obligation to bring together Local Offender Accommodation Forums in order to 'work towards improving and increasing the range of accommodation for offenders'. The work carried out under the initiative has been extensively researched and reported for example by Smith *et al.* (1993). While the authors draw attention to the real difficulties and variations which have been experienced in the organisation and working of the different Forums they also conclude that where practice has been good it has produced a real impact upon the range and quality of accommodation available for Probation Service clients.

Among that series of good practice examples, the Berkshire Offender Accommodation Strategy documents of 1990–3 and 1993–6 provide clear evidence of a local Service responding in a way far beyond an individual focus to the needs of its service users. Published in June 1990 the 1990–3 document reported a survey of November 1989 which revealed 332 homeless clients out of 1,460 cases (i.e. 23 per cent) surveyed and detailed plans to combat a chronic shortage of accommodation in the county, particularly for the under-25s. The 1993–6 document records both progress and setbacks experienced in meeting the original goals together with a new set of developmental priorities.

Local strategies are not in a position to solve all the accommodation problems faced by people who have been in trouble. Indeed many of their best efforts go into mitigating the effects of other more powerful actors in the field. The Berkshire document draws attention to the difficulties caused by delays in the local authority administration of housing benefit, the changes in Housing Association management allowances for special needs projects and planned changes in Home Office grants to voluntary sector projects (see Cheston *et al.*, 1991, for a more detailed account of these changes and their potential effects). The Strategy emphasises the effects of wider social policies, particularly the accommodation consequences of community care policies for the elderly and mentally vulnerable:

> The de-institutionalisation of the care of children, the elderly, the mentally ill and of offenders is a worthy aim that can only be achieved if accommodation and support in the community is available and affordable. The Berkshire Forum believes this will not happen in the foreseeable future, and that this will be at substantial cost to these individuals and to the community. (Berkshire Probation Service, 1993: 14)

Nor is Government, in its more direct involvement, unambiguously helpful. The introduction of the 1988 changes, and the development of the Probation Accommodation Grants scheme, was followed by the Criminal Justice Act 1991 which required local services to devote a proportion of budgets to grant aid to voluntary sector projects and, at the time of writing, by the devolution of the whole PAG scheme to local areas. While not undesirable in themselves, these changes inevitably alter the relationship between the Service and local partners. The formalising of grant relationships – through service level agreements, the introduction of new and additional performance and monitoring criteria and procedures – can provide greater clarity and firmer understanding of respective roles and obligation. It can also, however, undermine the intangible assets of good will and genuine partnership. It can also, as Avon, one of the pilot areas for devolution of the Probation Accommodation Grants scheme, discovered, have direct consequences in creating new conflicts of interest.

The 1988 scheme required local Services to nominate Senior Probation Officers to the management committees of voluntary projects in receipt of grants. Under the devolved version of the 1988 arrangements these same schemes are now funded – or not funded – by the direct decision of the local Service. The position of senior officers in this new way of proceeding is potentially untenable.

Despite these reservations, the coordinated, strategic approach to housing for offenders, as evidenced in the Berkshire documents, remains a clear example of positive action to address the problem which it identifies as being that 'homeless and poor housing conditions are closely related to offending'. In Avon, too, the picture is one of determination to build upon the strengths of partnership, preserving the advantages of the strategic approach and building upon it in the pursuit of flexible, affordable and accessible accommodation for its service users.

While the idea of 'partnership' can be problematic, where the Probation Service itself holds so many key cards, there are a number of other initiatives in the accommodation field where the Service has a legitimate interest, but where power and responsibility is more widely shared. The pressing need for the Service to take an active part in such developments is a general theme of this book and it is as true of the housing field as any of the forms of provision which we consider. Two practical examples have to suffice to illustrate the advantages which such an approach can engender. In Gloucestershire, a partnership between the Social Services Department of the County Council, the housing departments of the different district councils and the voluntary sector has set up a series of 'one-stop-shops' in which young people with accommodation needs can be assessed and assisted. The number of young people for whom previous experience of care or custody feeds into later accommodation difficulties is a growing problem in both rural and urban areas. The experience of being passed from one defensive organisation to another is one of the most off-putting which vulnerable people face in their dealings with the agencies of the welfare state. The Gloucestershire scheme aims to overcome this by bringing together, under one roof, the combined resources of those organisations which have responsibility in this area. Young people who have been in trouble are among the more prominent users of the new arrangement. The Probation Service, we argue, has lessons which can be learned from this sort of mutual and cooperative approach to service development.

The second example of such a way of attempting to improve provision for those in need can be found in 'Bond Bank' developments. The 1988 social security changes withdrew the previous capacity of the benefit system to pay 'bonds' through which access to private sector accommodation had normally to be secured. As with so many social policy changes of the past 15 years, time and energy has then to be devoted, by those in the field, to putting Humpty Dumpty back together again – sometimes even with the involvement of those who had helped to push him off the wall in the first place! Thus in Cardiff, the local City Council has been able to set up a 'Bond Bank', using money provided by the Welsh Office. The Bond Bank uses a pool of money to underwrite deposits normally required in cash by landlords. No money changes hands but the accommodation provider is issued with a certificate which guarantees against loss – through damage etc. – at the end of the tenancy. Mechanisms operate to assess the state of accommodation on offer at the start and to adjudicate upon any claim at the end of a tenancy. If money is paid out by the Bank it is recoverable from the individual tenant. There is no limit to the number of times people can apply for a bond on moving addresses, provided they have no claim for outstanding cash against them. The scheme aims to raise the standard and quality of private rented accommodation in the city as well as allowing people reliant on low incomes or state benefits the means of access to good quality secure rented housing. After the first year of the scheme's operation, the local Probation Service has invested funds with the Bank which is used to issue Bond Certificates specifically for probation clients in order for them to secure private rented accommodation.

Both the Gloucester and Cardiff schemes came into operation because of the concern of a group of workers daily facing the impossibility of gaining access to private sector accommodation for their clients. In Cardiff, probation officers were prominent among those who took part in an initial research and lobbying group which developed the scheme and persuaded the local authority to take it on. In the final part of this Commentary section we turn to a different example of work in the housing field which came from the individual efforts of a group of grass roots workers.

The Llamau Housing Society was born one day in October 1988 in the back room of a Torquay café. Three people, all then probation officers, had taken shelter there from the onset of the winter weather and, more especially, the inevitable 'are these boys with you?' enquiries which accompany any worthwhile youth hostelling project with young offenders. Among that group of young people were a range of individuals for whom four nights at a youth hostel represented the most settled period in their recent or foreseeable accommodation circumstances. Thinking about that fact, and the way in which vulnerable young people without that basic anchor are rendered all the more vulnerable and hence all the more disadvantaged in responding to the high expectation of responsible, contributing lives which are increasingly laid upon them, led the workers concerned to the conclusion that something must be done – and that they were going to do it!

A steering group was recruited with surprising ease and soon represented a range of individuals who had daily contact with the sort of difficulties faced by young people seeking to re-establish themselves in the community following – or under threat of – a period in care or custody. The group quickly set about addressing the essential issues of purpose, philosophy and a name sufficiently unpronounceable to arrest the attention of almost any funding body.

The purpose of the Society is to provide supported accommodation for young people in the 16–21 age range, where the absence of decent and affordable accommodation underlies other problems and particularly, offending or risk of offending.

The philosophy which motivates the Society centres around a commitment to the belief that a decent and affordable place to live should be an elementary right in any civilised society. Within that framework it aims for equal opportunity in selection and full participation in the progress of individuals through the Project by those individuals themselves.

Initial funding for the project came from Tai Cymru, the Housing Corporation for Wales, and the support of a variety of charitable Trusts. With this assistance a property was bought, converted into five independent bedsitter units and opened for business in August 1991. Today it has two houses in operation and a third well advanced in the planning process.

Llamau receives its referrals from statutory agencies in South Glamorgan, and from the Probation Service in particular. More than half the individuals advised and assisted by that Service itself in the year to March 1993 were from the 16–21 age group. The strategy document of the local accommodation forum acknowledged that homelessness and inadequate housing is a major contributory factor in re-offending behaviour.

In terms of strategic intervention a number of lessons may be drawn from the Project. In the short term it was important to have drawn together a broad based and hard-working group, prepared to learn and to be involved in all aspects of the project.

In the longer term attention has switched more to policy and procedure, attempting to ensure that services provided involve the young people as directly as possible in their own futures and offer them the best opportunity to avoid the damaging and destructive effects of entanglement in the criminal justice system. At the same time, survival and development has placed greater emphasis upon linking the project to wider provision, for example through Home Office funding and the local Social Services Department accommodation strategy.

The main message for this Commentary from the Llamau project lies in the grassroots quality of the initiative, coming as it did from probation officers, struggling with the offending careers of some deeply disadvantaged young people who recognised that the needs of those individuals could best be served by wider action. Llamau, as the other initiatives discussed in this Commentary, shows what can still be achieved in a cold climate.

6 Health

Joan Orme and Colin Pritchard

It is no longer enough, if it ever was, to think of the probation officer's job simply, or even mainly, in terms of advising, assisting and befriending, and of a casework relationship with an individual offender. (Faulkener, 1989: 4)

Introduction

When reflecting on the role of the Probation Service in dealing with health related issues it is arguable that the probation officer's job frequently extends beyond advising, assisting and befriending. The possibility of linking probation intervention with, for example, a condition for treatment, has existed for some time. Such conditions have required probation officers to play a significant role in liaising with the relevant services, imposing clear expectations on the person on supervision and acting as an intermediary between the health services and the criminal justice service. However recent research has shown that health related issues are not confined to those who have additional conditions in their probation order. The caseloads of probation officers include people who are poor, have chaotic lifestyles, and experience multiple problems. These psycho-social characteristics (Pritchard *et al.*, 1992) are frequently related to health issues. This chapter explores the evidence that there are in the majority of probation caseloads individuals who, either through their current offending behaviour or through life long disadvantage, present problems which relate to a substantial mental health dimension; health ramifications of drug/alcohol difficulties, and a higher likelihood of being exposed to HIV infection.

Additionally, in carrying out supervision, probation officers are constrained by the changes in the organisation of delivery of health care services. The emergence of hospital trusts and GP fundholding significantly affects access to health services for those whose lifestyle is chaotic or whose health situation is chronic and requires repeated treatment. While the Probation Service at area and national level will need to develop strategies based on partnership arrangements, the substantive activity will take place within the relationship between the individual probation officer and offender, and will include negotiating access to services and encouraging cooperation with relevant services providing treatment. This is part of a total management perspective, which goes beyond focusing on offending behaviour. In this chapter we will outline the ramifications of individual probation officers' involvement in working with health related problems. We will conclude by exploring possible models of organisation and intervention in relation to health issues.

Background

The specific health related responsibilities of the Probation Service are clearly identified in the Criminal Justice Act 1991 which continued the powers of the Court to require an offender whose mental condition requires it, to submit to medical treatment as a condition of a probation order. In addition paragraph 6 of schedule 1A provides for offenders who are dependent on, or who misuse, drugs or alcohol to be required to undergo treatment for their condition, where this is associated with their offending, as an additional requirement of a probation order. This necessitates a 'suitably-qualified person' satisfying the Courts that the offender is dependent on or misuses drugs or alcohol, that this contributed to the offence and that the offender's condition requires, or may respond to, treatment.

Such conditions may be seen to give probation officers the necessary mandate to intervene in specific health related issues. However, as Harding points out, the strength of the probation order lies 'not necessarily in the conditions which are attached to the order, either negative or restrictive, but in the substance of the agreement between the probation officer and the offender and the demands it makes on both parties' (1987: 7). These agreements, while initially focusing on individual relationships, increasingly have depended on liaison with other professionals, either within the criminal justice system, or in related fields of health and social care. The potential for creative partnerships has been underpinned by the Green Paper *Supervision and Punishment in the Community: A Framework for Action* (Home Office, 1990b). The emphasis here is on partnership with the voluntary and independent sectors concentrating on particular aspects of service provision. However the notion of 'supervision packages with the coordination of services provided by others' could well be extended to include health related services, whether or not there is a specific condition of the order. Such a mandate is not new: 'Good probation officers have to forge links with a range of formal services, including employers, youth training schemes, housing departments and associations, adult literacy schemes and specialist health care' (Harding, 1987: 6).

More significantly, other policy changes may indicate the need for the probation officer to be a more active advocate in the various social systems and health care provisions. The impact of community care policies for people with mental health problems has repercussions for the Probation Service. The greater number of people who have to cope in the community with limited resources leads to some being dealt with by the criminal Courts, often for petty offences, and there is a long-standing link between adverse socio-economic circumstances and a corresponding increase in mental hospital admissions, as well as increases in offences (Duster, 1995). In the absence of any other appropriate resource the probation officer is required to provide a service. Also those offenders who have a diagnosed mental health problem are not able to access appropriate services and are processed through the criminal justice system, appearing repeatedly on the caseloads of probation officers. Provision has to be made within hostels, but also individual probation officers often have to manage, control and contain mentally disturbed offenders both pre- and post-release from custody, and in attempts to divert from prison.

These changes are compounded by the cost-consciousness of the different parts of the NHS (Department of Health, 1992), precipitated by the purchaser/provider split, which has led to narrow focusing on local/departmental budgets and has inhibited collaboration. Over-speedy hospital discharges, swamping over-stretched community services, leads to greater readmission of the same patients, and an inflation in the statistics, as they are counted twice. The relevance of this to the Probation Service, is that fundholding GPs will perceive such patients as making inordinate demands. There is a financial disincentive to accept such people as new patients and a temptation to strike existing patients off lists, or resist referring them for treatment. The purchaser/provider split in the health service requires district health authorities to 'purchase' services for those living in the area. Clinics and hospitals are wary about treating people without a previously agreed contract with the relevant health authority. The implication for probation clients is that mobility/homelessness means that they are not always 'normally' relevant in a particular district, and therefore may not be covered by the contract. Also the nature of their problems means that they may benefit from a continuity of care which will not be available under the present arrangements, different 'episodes' of health care being provided by different units/health care teams. This means that the burden of providing continuity falls to the probation officer.

While such arguments are evident for those with mental health problems it is also likely that, in less dramatic ways, those on the caseloads of the Probation Service are disadvantaged in access to general health care. Low income, poor housing and ethnic background have contributed to inequalities in access to, and provision by the health service (Townsend and Davidson, 1982), and probation clients frequently experience this disadvantage. The overwhelming evidence comes from health orientated research, as poverty is associated with a whole range of poorer health status and lowered life expectancy (Whitehead, 1990). Ironically, the changes in the financial arrangements in the health service which may disadvantage probation clients are paralleled by one of the most progressive and community orientated initiatives for many years, namely *The Health of the Nation: A Strategy for England and Wales* (Department of Health, 1992). Targets, over time, have been set for different parts of the NHS, which have a particularly strong preventive focus in reducing avoidable deaths from, for example, coronary heart disease, strokes, lung cancer and suicide.

The focus on suicide is of particular significance to health issues for offenders. The links between suicide and unemployment, particularly among males, have been proven repeatedly (Dieskstra, 1989; Pritchard, 1992), but the offender–suicidal behaviour axis is also well documented (Dooley, 1990; Gunn *et al.*, 1991). Suicide rates may become 'a paradoxical indicator' of the effectiveness of the Community and Psychiatric Services and may well have an impact on the work of the Probation Service. A fall in the rate will be seen to indicate improvement in the Service while an increase in suicide, especially from the 1990 level, will be interpreted as the failure of the Services. The *Health of the Nation* initiative may well have negative implications for the Probation Service as insufficiently funded agencies seek to shuffle-off the blame, or over-focus on their own limited terms of reference, ignoring the ramifications of the interrelationship and interreaction of offending and mental disordered behaviour. At best, an alliance could substantially improve the service the citizen needs. At worst, probation officers might find themselves managing offenders with multiple health and social problems with limited access to services and presenting demanding behaviour including further offending.

Evidence

The current imperative for probation officers to confront offending behaviour operates on assumptions that offenders are in the first and last instance criminals, and that this is the only aspect of behaviour which will need the attention of professionals. However, the evidence that clients of the Probation Service represent the full range of social and medical problems is long standing. Davies's study identified 4.3 per cent of his sample of 17–20 year old males as experiencing ill health or physical disability to such an extent that the 'probation officer might have expected to find his [sic] casework seriously affected by it' (1969: 21). However, 20.8 per cent were assessed as 'disturbed', that is suffering from mental disturbance and 'some kind of inadequacy' (1969: 23). In contrast to present-day caseloads no specific mention is made of alcohol dependence and Davies found relatively few of his sample (7) had been convicted of drug related offences.

By 1982 the situation had changed. Offenders with alcohol related problems were featuring significantly in probation caseloads, as were people involved in drug abuse. Knapman's study of probation caseloads in Northamptonshire found 47 per cent of offenders had alcohol related problems (1982). A similar study in Hereford and Worcestershire (1982) while showing fewer offenders with alcohol related offences, demonstrated that alcohol related offences were almost as common for female offenders (22 per cent) as for males (28 per cent). These figures are repeated in the Humberside study (Taylor, 1986) which identified 33 per cent of all offenders as 'hard-core' problem drinkers.

Mental health problems

The finding that there was a significant level of relatively 'hidden' mental health problems in clients of the Probation Service should not be surprising as this reflects the Huxley study of clients of a northern Social Services Department (Huxley *et al.*, 1987). Typically, the psychiatric dimension was not the major difficulty and consequently the case would be 'categorised' and counted under a different single heading. Similarly a study undertaken of all those convicted of indictable offences by a city Magistrates' Court and Crown Court in 1983 (Shepherd, 1990) identifies the extent of mental health problems in probation caseloads. Of the total sample of 2,588 people, 15 per cent were identified as having suffered from a psychiatric disorder within ten years of conviction and 181 (7 per cent of the total) within 12 months of conviction. The findings that 14 per cent of all males convicted and 20 per cent of females were 'disordered' need to be understood in the context of the double jeopardy experienced by women involved in offending behaviour, which leads to assumptions that they are 'mad not bad' (Heidensohn, 1987). Nevertheless they indicate the extent of probation officers' involvement with offenders who experience problems with their mental health. Details of the case register revealed that the disordered were significantly more likely to be already known to the Probation Service at conviction and more likely to have been in prison at sometime. These findings, together with the fact that the disordered were significantly more likely to be put on probation (13 per cent compared with 8 per cent of the non-disordered), support the notion that they are likely to figure significantly in the caseloads of probation officers. In addition the findings that the disordered were more likely to breach orders, be convicted of alcohol related offences and have more court appearances during the sample year indicates that they contributed significantly to the workloads of probation officers.

The workload implications are further supported by Shepherd's comparison of 135 probation clients who were identified as 'mentally disordered', compared with an equal sample of matched controls who were not disordered. The disordered were less likely to have any social support systems such as partners, children or contact with first degree relatives. As Shepherd concludes 'they are therefore a major responsibility for the Probation Service. However, they are difficult clients in that they are more likely to breach the various orders to which they are subject' (1990: 3). The findings that probation officers carried out more interviews, wrote and received more letters, reports and memoranda and made and received more telephone calls in connection with the disordered offenders than with the non-disordered suggests that the work in supervising offenders with a history of mental illness requires intervention which involves more than simply focusing on offending behaviour.

General health problems

Equally revealing is the recent evidence that in the totality of probation officers' caseloads the incidence of health related problems is high. A survey of 214 'ordinary' probation clients (i.e. they were not identified by any particular offence, intervention or specific problem) between the ages of 18 and 35 years old (Pritchard *et al.*, 1992) identified four health related problem areas: illegal drug use (35 per cent), alcohol (46 per cent), HIV risk (15 per cent) and mental health problems (21 per cent). A measure of the extent of the mental health problems is that 15 per cent of the sample had been treated for depression, 6 per cent for mental illness and 14 per cent of the sample had been involved in attempted suicide.

The group in the sample with alcohol related problems experienced greater poverty, and had higher long-term unemployment; more money and debt difficulties and chronic housing problems. The correlation is possible either way, alcohol abuse contributing to the problems or the problems aggravating the abuse of alcohol. All of which demonstrates that intervention by a probation officer, which aims merely to challenge offending behaviour, is likely to have little impact on underlying factors which might contribute to that offending behaviour.

HIV risk

Most significantly the poverty experienced by the sample, while to some extent expected, was linked by the authors to illegal drug/alcohol misuse and in turn to HIV risk behaviour (defined as casual sexual pick-ups/promiscuity). The interrelationship of illegal drug misuse and alcohol problems with HIV risk behaviour causes them to comment that 'the range of problems indicates a considerable degree of psycho-social turmoil, suggesting people whose psycho-social judgement might be impaired' (Pritchard *et al.*, 1992: 238).

The continuing involvement of the Probation Service in prison work and after-care raises other health issues. The drug related behaviour and the failure of the English prison system to tackle positively the HIV risk behaviour in prisons (Verboud and Padel, 1992) lead to prisoners being discharged with need for support and care. Verboud and Padel (1992) point out that many offenders who have a drug problem when they enter prison continue the habit. A number of studies have shown that single homeless people not only consist of a substantial subgroup of mentally ill people, but also people who have been in prison (Vagg, 1992). Additionally, studies of unemployed homeless have identified pressure for some to become involved in drug distribution, crime and prostitution (Pritchard and Clooney, 1994). Therefore, because of their contact with offenders involved in drug misuse, poverty and homelessness, probation officers are perhaps *more* likely to meet clients at risk of HIV infection than other agencies.

The links between health related problems and poverty may be masked by referrals for financial or other reasons which may have significance for female offenders. Studies which concentrate on offending behaviour and employment ignore the dimension of offending behaviour by women, many of whom will not be employed. They will also fail to address those aspects of women's lives which contribute to their isolation and specific mental health problems. This has led to a focusing on female offenders as being doubly deviant and to a concentration on health related issues for female offenders as being related to their physiological and biological needs (Luckhaus, 1982).

Pritchard and his colleagues (1992) also found that clients of the Probation Service had significant overt contact with health agencies. Nearly a third (28 per cent) had been involved with their GP, 13 per cent with a psychiatrist while 9 per cent had had hospital inpatient treatment and 6 per cent outpatient treatment, and this among an age group who are expected to be at their most healthy. This should dispel the notion that clients of the Probation Service are offenders first and last, and also suggests that if there is to be a meaningful intervention in the individual's life which might contribute to the cessation of offending then individual probation officers and the Probation Service need to have significant liaison with health professionals.

Implications for the work of the Service

Currently it would seem that the work of the Probation Service is concerned with challenging offending behaviour, not with improving the quality of life, but as Hill suggests 'the process of helping offenders improve their overall quality of life within communities may be instrumental in creating conditions necessary for reducing crime' (1987: 238). Specifically, the implication of a policy imperative which focuses on offending behaviour is that health risks will be ignored, or that further offending will be precipitated by health related problems, especially if health related problems include drug and alcohol misuse.

The need for probation officers to go 'beyond offending behaviour' is clearly identified in Knapman's study (1982) which found that probation officers identified only 17 per cent of the 47 per cent of offenders who had alcohol related problems. More significantly offenders themselves might not link their offending to their drinking. There is therefore a need for training and patterns of working which both equip the Probation Service and challenge those with alcohol related problems (Purser, 1987). During the 1980s the proliferation of projects related to alcohol education, drink drivers and multiple life problems demonstrated the potential for effective work in the area of drink related offending (Purser, 1987). These have taken place at the level of individual and group intervention but Purser argues for the Probation Service to join fora at a national level and identify with initiatives to force change in governmental attitudes; this is dependent on policy initiatives involving partnership and particularly at a local level where the notion of partnership can operate both to provide interventions and to address prevention. Such partnerships with voluntary initiatives, together with statutory health care, also require cooperation with those in the criminal justice field in order to identify and work towards a consistent approach to alcohol related crime. Interestingly, the very criticisms which the Government has made of the Probation Service as a system of fragmented out-of-touch workers operating in their specialist functions which fails to treat the offender as a whole person are contained within a message about the need for the Probation Service to be involved in 'assembling packages, co-ordinating services provided by others and seeing that collectively they achieve the right results' (Faulkener, 1989: 7).

In many senses the probation officer as manager of packages of supervision in the community is not a new phenomenon, but what is being argued is that it can take a number of forms and have different sets of implications both for individual workers and for the organisation of Service delivery. The involvement of professionals and para-professionals from other agencies in, for example, alcohol education courses is a model already adopted by the

Probation Service, but it still necessitates the involvement of the Probation Service because of its particular understanding of, and expertise in, issues of offending behaviour and the criminal justice system.

Partnership arrangements with health services and voluntary agencies are fundamental to the work of the Service and, at one level, are not new. What could be innovative are models of cooperation which include, for example, seconded officers to community drug teams and community alcohol teams. This could be creative in acknowledging the expertise in working with offenders with these problems set alongside the expertise of health and voluntary agency staff whose experience stems from wider interests of alcohol and drug problems in the community and the public at large, providing links with the criminal justice system. If it is unrealistic to expect the Probation Service to have expertise in everything it is unrealistic to expect other agencies to have expertise in offending behaviour.

More significantly research evidence suggests that such partnership arrangements should not only be staffed by the Probation Service, but managed by them. A recent study revealed that probation officers 'topped the league table' of helpful professionals in the opinion of a sample of homeless who had had recent contact with the Service (Cox and Pritchard, 1995). An examination of over one hundred current clients of the Dorset Probation Service revealed that clients valued authoritative information, direct help with practical matters, support with personal and family difficulties, all based upon trust, confidence and an individualised service going beyond a focus on offending behaviour (Ford *et al.*, 1995).

In looking to the literature of care management and community care for models of organisation and management of packages of supervision, Fulwood (1989) finds that partnership does not obviate the need for the professionally qualified worker, whose training includes the solid base of knowledge, values and skills which has been consistently identified with the practice of social work. It is this very base that has ensured that the Probation Service received such positive acclaim in the consumer surveys mentioned above.

Conclusion

Supervision and Punishment in the Community acknowledged individual supervision to be 'an important and valuable part of the service's professional equipment' (Home Office, 1990b: 7). Significantly further guidance and directives contained in national standards concentrate on the mechanics of the supervisory process, with little acknowledgement of the implications for the content of the supervision process. We have demonstrated that health related problems are likely to be the focus of probation intervention, either because they are directly related to offending behaviour, or because the life circumstances of those involved in criminal activity are going to require attention to health related matters.

The responsibility for ensuring that the Probation Service is equipped to deal with such issues rests with management at local and national level. The responsibility for identifying and working with the problems rests with individual officers, both in their supervision of offenders and in the writing of pre-sentence reports. However, arrangements require more than an acknowledgement that facilities have to be set up or accessed; the demands of probation clients are unpredictable. The various reviews of systems to measure and codify the probation task have attempted to reflect the work-load demands identified by Shepherd (1990). However, the current initiatives to deprofessionalise the Service fail to acknowledge that the health related problems of offenders are not always obvious and assessable at the point of contact with the criminal justice system. It is important to have specialist provision, either residential or day care, for specific problems (e.g. alcohol or drug related behaviour), but it is equally important that probation officers have training which helps them to recognise and deal with some of the ways in which those specific health problems manifest themselves, the ways health issues can impact upon social behaviour and the degree to which social and economic conditions can exacerbate health problems. Such training would need to acknowledge the different health experiences of women and men and the health risks faced by people from different ethnic backgrounds. Equally, in monitoring the work of probation officers it is essential that acknowledgement is given to the specific interventions that health related problems might create. These could vary from referral to drug and alcohol services to time consuming advocacy, on an individual basis, with local health services and their management bodies. Hence addressing the health needs of those on probation will require not only innovative community based resources, but appropriately trained generalist probation practitioners who have the capacity in their workloads to respond to the conditions in the lives of individuals and identify and manage a coherent range of resources.

Editors' commentary

In arguing for a broader strategy to address the health related problems of probation clients, the authors of this chapter have highlighted research findings which demonstrate the extent of those problems. A significant majority of those clients face the closure of opportunities which would have the effect of improving their lifestyle and their health; moreover, they experience the double jeopardy of having multiple health problems and being disadvantaged in access to health care. Interestingly, the birth of the probation ideal can be traced back to an involvement with health problems related to alcohol consumption, although the concern of police court missionaries was with the health of the soul! Modern probation officers, as Orme and Pritchard argue, in their concern to help people to reduce their offending cannot ignore the health of the mind and body.

The context for the required shift in emphasis is shaped partly by the concept of partnership, and the impact of community care policies; within that context there is a need for a change in both management and practitioner perspective. As Lloyd puts it: 'Whilst we may be in the system, we do not have to be exclusively of it' (1989: 25). For managers that change might be about formulating policies which are premised on the notion of joint strategic frameworks involving other agencies and bodies; the provision of resources and the support of practice initiated within those frameworks; an organisational culture which embraces that practice; and the provision of training for practitioners that will provide them with the required skills and knowledge. For practitioners, the requisite change might be a widening of perspective, an emphasis on systems intervention, and working alongside clients to effect change in others.

In attempting to illustrate how a change in emphasis might look in practice, we have drawn on a few examples of innovative work in the area of health; what follows is a descriptive outline of the work and a commentary. The first, in the field of mental health, is an interesting example of a Court diversion scheme in Mid Glamorgan based on cooperation between a Forensic Unit, the Probation Service, the Police, Clerks of the Courts, Social Services and the Crown Prosecution Service who all make up the membership of the project steering group: they also hold responsibility for its evaluation.

The project, which began in 1994, emanated from the concerns of the Forensic Unit (which incorporated a senior probation officer in its team) about the numbers of mentally disordered people ending up in custody. Its funds are drawn partly from the Home Office, and partly from a national health trust. At the time of writing, the staffing of the project consists of two community psychiatric nurses who cover the Courts in two of the valley towns. The project will be evaluated at the end of 12 months and a report presented to the Home Office.

The workers operate a four-tier strategy which involves interviewing to ensure that mentally disordered offenders are not remanded in custody, exploring the public interest dimension, and in harness with the Crown Prosecution Service, diverting from prosecution where appropriate. In addition, the workers interview in post-custodial situations to arrange bail, and in conjunction with all of these develop a package of care arrangements. These interventions may involve either negotiation with the police before a formal charge has been made, or with the Crown Prosecution Service after the person has been formally charged. In both these situations a consultant and/or probation officer may work with the community psychiatric nurse. A typical intervention package can involve a bed at the local psychiatric unit, plus additional and coordinated support provided by the Community Mental Health Team, Social Services and Probation.

So what is the Probation Service's involvement in this? As we have already indicated, a senior probation officer is located in the Forensic Unit, and there is a probation presence on the steering group. Management support is evident, and at a practice level probation officers are involved in the review of cases with the community psychiatric nurse, joint cell interviews, representations to the Court, and general proactive work with those mentally disordered people who are remanded in custody. To this extent the Service is moving towards the type of cooperation with health and social services proposed by Dorothy Tonak (1992) who advocates a strategy which exploits the legislative framework provided by the Criminal Justice Act 1991. More specifically she suggests a focus on the provision of information to the Court, liaison between medical practitioners and probation officers, dialogue with officials, exploitation of the Section 96 provision of grants to those provided with bail, and the use of Section 27 to strengthen guardianship orders.

It seems to us that the Probation Service can also play a vital role in ensuring a sense of ownership by the Courts through exploiting its existing networks and unique relationships within the Court system. Specific policy statements may also increase the degree of ownership within the Service itself, particularly if they include a commitment to team specialists and joint training.

The success of a scheme such as that in Mid Glamorgan depends, in our view, on the degree to which it involves probation staff; the extent to which it is linked to housing in the community (and not simply hospital beds); and the avoidance of reliance on a narrowly defined medical model in the diagnosis of a person's problems. Nevertheless, the Mid Glamorgan scheme is an interesting example of work which can achieve a significant impact in the way the criminal justice system responds to the mentally disordered who appear before the Court. It fits the pioneering model of broader public interest case assessment in Inner London (Stone, 1989) which itself has demanded new skills and techniques of officers more used to exploring the difficulties which may have led to the committing of offences. Instead, the officers adjusted technique in order to obtain relevant information without touching on the alleged offence. Similarly, working alongside community psychiatric nurses and consultants and towards aims other than dealing with offending, requires adjustment in perspective as well as enhancement of skills and knowledge (Hudson *et al.*, 1993). The importance of integrating such practice into the probation repertoire is underlined by the outcome of research into the experience of mentally disordered female remand prisoners in Holloway undertaken by a research team from the Cambridge Institute of

Criminology (Dell *et al.*, 1993). They found that 68 per cent of the women were discharged from the prison on Section 37 hospital orders, a fact that challenged the need for them to be in custody in the first place.

As Orme and Pritchard have emphasised, another growing area of concern for probation officers working in the casualty ward of post-Thatcherite Britain is the misuse of drugs and alcohol and its attendant social and personal problems. It is a practice area in which there are a growing number of examples of initiatives which are based on a broader vision of the contribution that the Service can make to ameliorate those problems. For the purposes of illustration, we shall elaborate on two of the most significant elements of emerging strategy – harm reduction and diversion from prison.

A specific harm reduction unit was set up by the Inner London Probation Service and provides a useful template (Boother, 1991). It is also interesting because it encompasses a dual approach which is designed to help individuals and have an impact on the social environment. Founded on research which explored current practice and the extent of the problem, the project incorporates a harm reduction objective which is directly supported by policy. The rationale for this policy lies in an acknowledgement of the complexity of drug taking activity; the nature of the problems faced by users trying to change their drug use pattern; and the importance of working towards achievable goals. This policy informs a strategy that includes networking with other agencies (and in particular, community drug teams), informing and attempting to influence the Courts, and practice that is premised on a user-centred perspective. As a consequence, the principles of eschewing any assumption about the desirability of being 'drug free' and respecting the user's right to identify desirable changes, are an inherent part of practice. The work also involves contact and liaison with other services, the promotion of the use of safer equipment, needle exchange facilities, and a commitment to the concept of phased withdrawal.

There are close similarities in this project with the approach taken by the South Sefton team in Merseyside which has been functioning for the past five years (Merseyside Probation Service, 1994). The team, which is comprised of counsellors from Social Services, a consultant psychiatrist, a community psychiatric nurse and drug counsellors from the Health Authority, and a probation officer and two Probation Service officers, is accountable to a joint management team. Although specialist staff are now in place in every division, the pattern of service still varies; so regular meetings of the probation managers of the drug specialists and the Merseyside Probation Service Drugs Advisory Group are held with an Assistant Chief Officer. Service ownership and commitment to the provision of resources which are key elements of successful projects (Andrews *et al.*, 1990) have made a significant contribution to the survival of the project.

As well as the needle and syringe exchange, hepatitis B vaccinations, and same day HIV testing, there are two features of this project worthy of closer attention. The first is the introduction of a GP liaison scheme which was accepted by the Mersey Regional Health Authority in 1993. Two team members have had half of their time freed up to work directly with the GPs under the auspices of a steering group that includes a pharmaceutical adviser, a GP adviser, a business manager from the North Mersey Trust, and a member of the Community Drugs Team. Attention has been paid to protocols and respective responsibilities and an initial agreement has been reached to test the scheme in a small number of practices where there is a large population of drug users. In this way probation officers are directly involved with the key people in the treatment network. The second is the commitment to risk reduction, and its differentiation from harm reduction; the former is defined as a concern with the totality of a person's lifestyle rather than just health. Members of the Sefton team recognise the potential for discomfort in an approach that might involve encouraging a user to substitute one illegal activity for another, but they persuasively argue that it is a prerequisite for effective intervention. Safe injecting, safe sex and the prescription of oral methadone are components of risk reduction but it might also include encouraging users to change from Temazepam to a less harmful, though still illegal if not prescribed, drug such as Valium.

Within a broad strategy there is, of course, a place for programmes that are specifically aimed at reducing consumption of drugs like alcohol, a commendable example of which is the alcohol related offending programme run by the Middlesex Probation Service's Special Programmes Unit. Designed for people whose offending is both serious and alcohol related, the programmes are supported by specialist voluntary agencies, and include a focus on alcohol and health, the influence of alcohol on crime, the social impact of alcohol, victims, and alcohol and driving. Ultimately the programme aims to provide participants with strategies for change, but crucial to that is follow-up support by the supervising officers. That might seem like stating the obvious but the failure to integrate the work of special programmes and subsequent supervision remains a prominent problem in probation work.

It is in these areas then that management support and endorsement is clearly of paramount importance, and perhaps provides the litmus test of any Service's commitment to move beyond offending behaviour and into the chaotic lifestyles of significant numbers of clients: without it practitioners will be unable to take the inherent risks. Above all else, it is the existence of clear policy which marks out the Inner London and Merseyside initiatives as examples to follow.

The second strand of the emerging strategy in relation to the health problems of probation clients is diversion from custody. We know that the cultures of prisons mirror the cultures outside their walls in their hierarchies and structures, and more particularly, in their constructions of deviant lifestyles. If you are criminally minded, and like illicit sex, violence, alcohol and other drugs there is no better place to go than one of Her Majesty's prisons; they are also the place to go to increase your chances of becoming HIV positive. In arguing for, and elucidating a medical paradigm of care for prisoners with HIV/AIDS, Thomas and Costigan (1992), graphically illuminate how dangerous a health hazard a prison is for even the averagely healthy prisoner; for more vulnerable groups it is worse.

It is against this background that Collinson (1991) highlights the failure of non-custodial responses to keep heroin users out of custody, and respond positively to the challenge presented by HIV and Aids. In so doing he delineates a range of structural problems within the Probation Service itself. For instance, while informal and voluntary programmes can be successful in addressing health problems, they often fail to persuade magistrates away from custodial responses to heroin linked offenders; however, on the other hand excessive conditional orders can be inappropriately matched to chaotic lifestyles. The lessons that can be learned from the experiences of the Inner London and Merseyside teams, and indeed from the parallel work in the field of mentally disordered offenders, are ripe for application to the specific objective of keeping vulnerable groups out of custody. In this respect, as Raynor has argued in Chapter 2, pre-sentence report writing is a critical practice area.

7 Conclusion

Mark Drakeford and Maurice Vanstone

We began this book by arguing that the Probation Service is not paying sufficient attention to the context of crime; and that a concern for chaotic lifestyles
ought, at least, to be balanced by a concern about the stage upon which those
lifestyles are acted out. In doing so, we acknowledged the positive steps taken
by the Service towards more empirically informed practice, and through our
commentaries we have attempted to highlight examples of work which go
beyond an individual focus: to this extent the book is optimistic. Living and
working in South Wales we have drawn a series of practice examples from
our own locality in the belief that similar initiatives are to be discovered in
other parts of Britain. We also chose five areas which while they represent
critical structural problems faced by probation clients, are not meant to be
exclusive. Hopefully, the contributions to the book have shown that the
discriminatory dimensions to those structural problems need a clear focus in
their own right or, to put it another way, that they have given sufficient cogni-
sance to the reality that to be poor, unemployed, homeless and ill in addition
to being black, female, gay or disabled will heighten the disadvantage experienced. Indeed, without any claim to originality, the basic tenet of the book is
that without social justice, criminal justice is not possible.

However, the book begins with Peter Raynor's succinct analysis of the way
in which the Probation Service is, and ought to be, influencing the criminal
justice system. In our Commentary on his chapter we highlighted how Youth
Court work has increased the need for a renewed systems approach based on
the dramatically successful juvenile justice system strategies of the 1970s and
1980s. In addition, we illustrated the potential of a systems intervention
approach in the areas of bail information and the Fines Court; the former
being important because of how early decisions in the judicial process affect
later ones, and the latter because of the renewed financial pressure on probation clients caused by the untimely demise of the unit fines system. This, we

103

suggested, is an area in which the Service's information technology can be used to its full potential.

In our Commentary on Chapter 3, we suggested a three part anti-poverty strategy for Probation Services set against a backdrop of research findings which tell us that practical help is highly valued by probation clients. The first strand relates to how Probation Services deploy their own resources, and spend their money. It seems to us that the likely effect upon already disadvantaged probation clients of such decisions will be at the forefront of thinking in Services that are committed to the non-discriminatory provision of help. The second strand, we have argued, is reliant on intervention which takes as its starting point that those agencies charged with the responsibility to dispense welfare benefits are hostile to the needs of poor people. Welfare rights work, therefore, has to be refocused on determined advocacy. The final strand of the strategy that we have suggested involves an extension of collaboration with those community initiatives such as credit unions, and cooperative buying schemes. In doing this, Services will be supporting directly activity which reduces the financial problems of probation clients, and thereby lessens one of the main pressures to offend.

Chapter 4 underlined the pivotal position of employment in relation to the risk of offending, and we drew attention to the individualised nature of much of the work of the Service on employment. While we acknowledged the continuing relevance of that individual work, we advocated a broader strategy which incorporated a particular focus on the needs of women, and black men and women, and which necessitates the harnessing of the power of the agency in lobbying and campaigning. We suggested, furthermore, that that power needs to be augmented by the existing power of the TECs, APEX and NACRO.

As we saw from Gill Stewart's optimistic chapter on housing it is an area in which the Probation Service, in cooperation with others, has made very significant progress. Our Commentary, while drawing attention to the ambiguity of a Government position which on the one hand, advocates action on homelessness, and on the other hand, closes hostels, featured potent and successful local initiatives. At a Service level these included the Berkshire Offending Accommodation Strategy; at a team level, the combination of practical help and development work; and at the informal level, groups of workers from different agencies who have developed independent community initiatives from scratch. In these ways much has been achieved despite the growing constraints on housing provision.

The theme of strategic responses is repeated in our Commentary on Joan Orme and Colin Pritchard's chapter on health, but with added emphasis on collaboration with others. As with housing this is an area of work in which the Probation Service is beginning to make progress, and there are models of good practice. We put forward three directions for the Service to take. First, towards diversion from prosecution and custody, particularly in the field of mental health but also in that of general public interest. Second, harm (and/or risk) reduction, and again, diversion from custody in the area of misuse of drugs, and finally the addressing of structural problems within the Probation Service itself (in particular, the increase in the use of conditional orders).

It is essential to the success of the Probation Service's efforts to address these difficult but tractable problems, that management gives weight to these efforts which is equal to the weight it has given to influencing individuals. Achieving that is only possible, in our view, if area management teams treat Home Office interventions as general guides as opposed to specific prescriptions. In this way, they can protect staff from the whims of politically ambitious Home Secretaries, and the worst effects of the growing bureau-cratisation of the Service. Furthermore, they will need to nurture developing expertise in these areas while also assessing and providing as far as they can the required resources. More than anything else, however, they will need to increase the campaigning and lobbying activities of the Service. It almost goes without saying that management activity likely to be most effective in redressing the balance will be premised on a collaborative rather than a macho style of management.

It is, the reader may well be thinking, easy to write about practice, but another matter to do it especially in the inclement economic and political weather of the 1990s. As editors we agree, and in so doing recognise that there are a number of issues and problems emanating from the kind of approach advocated in this book. We hope, that the combination of the broad overviews in the chapters and our commentaries on the practical implica-tions, provides sufficient pointers to their resolution. However, we have so far not dwelled for too long on the concept of partnership. Two recent analyses (Smith *et al.*, 1993; James and Bottomely, 1994) helpfully throw some light on the emerging problems while at the same time, pinpointing the lessons to be learned. Smith and his co-authors provide a positive reminder of the lengthy experience of the Probation Service in partnerships through its involvement with the voluntary sector and accommodation, the Prison Service and Community Service Volunteers, and the experience in the community super-vision of juvenile offenders. In a clearly optimistic analysis they nevertheless raise some important caveats.

In questioning whether or not it is possible for the tasks of probation staff to be neatly divided into core tasks and others, they raise the prospect of proba-tion officers becoming case managers. They imply (and given the title of this book this *would* be ironic) that it could leave staff concentrating exclusively on offending while partnership agencies address the broader problems. The idea is reminiscent of Robert Harris's proposed division of core tasks (1980). Our argument is very different. If probation officers are to help people avoid offending it is vital that they retain their face-to-face work with their clients, and form 'action systems' with them (Pincus and Minahan, 1973).

A further problem is that of accountability: Smith and his colleagues correctly point out that as more activity is hived off the greater becomes the anxiety of the Service and the risk that it resorts to more and more bureaucratic procedures. James and Bottomley expand on this problem by helpfully underlining the critical nature of the balance between central prescription and response to local issues. Both analyses develop this point to exemplify the potential for destructive clashes over unresolved power struggles and unclarified values and principles.

We draw the book to a close with a list of good practice prescriptions for effective partnership or interagency work extrapolated from both accounts of what can go wrong:

1   Clear statements of values, aims and interests.
2   Proper coordination of both internal and external resourcing (this will necessitate agreed management responsibilities and tasks, pooling of resources, agreed communication channels, and mutual trust).
3   Allowing time for the initiatives to develop and grow.
4   Effective monitoring not only of outcomes, but also of the impact of initiatives on the parties involved.
5   An agreed problem-solving approach to decision-making.
6   The avoidance of an over-formalised 'contracting culture' which excludes less structured street agencies.

For the Probation Service to have the right to expect its clients to assume some responsibility for their lives, it has itself to accept its responsibility to make interventions on behalf of those clients and stand alongside them. During the past ten years or so, it has made considerable progress in developing stratagems and programmes to help those clients change. We hope that this book has made a small contribution to helping the Service to effect changes in their economic and social circumstances as well. We hope that it has achieved that by reminding us that offending behaviour strategies, when narrowly conceived and mechanistically delivered detach offending from those factors which make it intelligible. It is implicit in such strategies that it is individuals who must change despite their deprivations, and their awareness of injustice and the crimes of the rich.

Social work in the criminal justice system should be about imaginatively helping individuals to change, and it should be concerned with the reduction of harm caused by crime. But it should also be about doing good in the lives of people who are themselves often deeply disadvantaged and whose life chances have already been damaged by poverty and poor quality, residual public services. It means re-embracing social explanations of crime which contribute to an understanding of the complexity of real people, leading real lives. In the process it means abandoning some of the false simplicities of the justice model which suggest that the range of choices, and the moral context in which choices are made, are the same for the company director as for the young person living in the broken down car parked on the forecourt of his parents' home on the Ely estate in Cardiff. Dissatisfaction, disaffection and the loss of hope of improvement are poor soil in which to help people lead law-abiding lives. If it is to be otherwise it means recreating a stake in society for those who are excluded. For probation officers this begins with understanding, explaining and seeking to improve the social circumstances of those people with whom the Probation Service works.

References

Advisory Council on the Penal System (1970) *Non-Custodial and Semi-Custodial Penalties*, London: HMSO.

Andrews, D.A., Zinger, I., Hode, R.D., Bonta, J., Genreau, P. and Cullen, F.T. (1990) 'Does correctional treatment work? A clinically relevant and psychologically informed meta-analysis', *Criminology*, **28**, 369–404.

Apex Trust (1993) *Apex Trust Report 1990 to 1992*, London: Apex Trust.

Association of Chief Officers of Probation (1989) *Employment Issues: Guidelines for Practice*, London: Association of Chief Officers of Probation.

Association of Chief Officers of Probation (1993) *Statistics on Employment Status of Offenders in the Community*, London: Association of Chief Officers of Probation.

Association of Chief Officers of Probation (1994) *Pre-Trial Services Working Group: Initiative to Develop Inter-Agency Pre-Trial Services*, London: Association of Chief Officers of Probation.

Bailey, R. and Ward, D. (1993) *Probation Supervision: Attitudes to Formalised Help*, Centre for Social Action, University of Nottingham.

Barclay, G.C. (1993) *Digest 2: Information on the Criminal Justice System in England and Wales*, London: Home Office Research and Statistics Department.

Becker, S. and Silburn, R. (1990) *The New Poor Clients*, Nottingham University Benefits Research Unit/Community Care, Surrey.

Berkshire Probation Service (1993) *Berkshire Offender Accommodation Strategy 1993–96*, Berkshire Probation Service.

Boother, M. (1991) 'Drug misuse: developing a harm reduction policy', *Probation Journal*, **38** (2), 75–80.

Boshier, R. and Johnson, D. (1974) 'Does conviction affect employment opportunities?', *British Journal of Criminology*, **14** (3), 264–8.

Boswell, G., Davies, M. and Wright, A. (1993) *Contemporary Probation Practice*, Aldershot: Avebury.

Bottoms, A.E. (1977), 'Reflections on the renaissance of dangerousness', *Howard Journal*, **16**, 70–97.

Box, S. (1987) *Recession, Crime and Punishment,* London: Macmillan.

Brenner, M.H. (1976a) *Estimating the Social Cost of National Economic Policy: Implications for Mental and Physical Health and Criminal Aggression,* Joint Economic Committee, Congress of the United States, Washington, DC: US Government Printing Office.

Brenner, M.H. (1976b) 'Time Series Analysis – effects of the economy on criminal behaviour and the administration of criminal justice (analysis of data from the United States, Canada, England, Wales and Scotland)', *in Economic Crises and Crime,* Rome: United Nations Social Defence Research Institute.

Brewer, C. and Lait, J. (1980) *Can Social Work Survive?* London: Temple Smith.

Broad, B. (1991) *Punishment Under Pressure: The Probation Service in the Inner City,* London: Jessica Kingsley.

Broad, B. and Denny, D. (1992) 'Citizenship, rights and the probation service: a question of empowering or oppressing probation service users', *Probation Journal*, **3** (4), 170–4.

Brody, S.R. (1976) *The Effectiveness of Sentencing,* London: HMSO.

Brown, A. and Crisp, C. (1992) 'Diverting cases from prosecution in the public interest', *Home Office Research Bulletin*, **32**, 7–12.

Buickhuisen, W. and Hoekstra, H.A. (1974) 'Factors related to recidivism', *British Journal of Criminology*, **14** (1), 63–9.

Canton, R. (1993) 'The Criminal Justice Act: trying to make sense of it all', *Napo News*, **44**, 7–9.

Central Statistical Office (1994) *Social Trends 24,* London: HMSO.

Cheston, L., Day, N. and Johnson, C. (1991) 'Ex-offender hostels: all change', *Probation Journal*, **38** (4), 186–9.

Chief Inspector of Prisons (1985) *The Preparation Of Prisoners for Release,* London: Home Office.

Chief Inspector of Probation (1993) *Annual Report 1993,* London: HMSO.

Cleveland Probation Service (1993) *Community Development Unit Annual Report,* Cleveland Probation Service.

Cochrane, D. (1989) 'Poverty, probation and empowerment', *Probation Journal*, **36** (4), 177–82.

Collinson, M. (1991) 'Keeping heroin users out of prison', *Probation Journal*, **38** (1), 20–4.

Commission on Social Justice (1993) *Social Justice in a Changing World,* London: IPPR/Rivers Oram Press.

Cook, D. and Hudson, B. (1993) *Racism and Criminology,* London: Sage.

Cornish, D. and Clarke, R. (1986) *The Reasoning Criminal: Rational Choice Perspectives in Offending,* London: Allen and Unwin.

Cox, M. and Pritchard, C. (1995) 'Troubles come not singly but in battalions: the pursuit of social justice in probation practice', in D. Ward and M. Lacey (eds), *Probation: Working for Justice*, London: Birch and Whiting.

Craig, G. and Glendinning, C. (1990) *Missing the Target*, London: Barnardos.

Crow, I.D. (1979) *Back Into Society: A Report on the Resettlement of Discharged Prisoners*, London: NACRO.

Crow, I.D. and Simon, F. (1987) *Unemployment and Magistrates' Courts*, London: NACRO.

Crow, I.D., Richardson, P., Riddington, C. and Simon, F. (1989) *Unemployment, Crime and Offenders*, London: Routledge.

Davies, M. (1969) *Probationers in their Social Environment*, Home Office Research Studies No. 2, London: HMSO.

Davies, M. (1974) *Social Work in the Environment*, Home Office Research Studies No. 21, London: HMSO.

Davies, M. (1981) *The Essential Social Worker*, London: Heinemann.

Day, N. (1988) 'Area accommodation strategies: a partnership approach to housing for homeless offenders', *Probation Journal*, **35** (3), 110–13.

Dean, H. and Taylor Gooby, P. (1992) *Dependency Culture: The Explosion of a Myth*, Hemel Hempstead: Harvester Wheatsheaf.

De Haan, W. (1990) *The Politics of Redress: Crime, Punishment and Penal Abolition*, London: Unwin Hyman.

Dell, S., Robertson, G., James, K. and Grounds, A. (1993) 'Remands and psychiatric assessment in Holloway Prison', *Journal of Psychiatry*, **163**, 634–44.

Denny, D. (1992) *Racism and Anti-Racism in Probation*, London: Routledge.

Department of Employment (1993a) 'Ethnic origins and the labour market', *Employment Gazette*, **101** (2), 25–43.

Department of Employment (1993b) *Employment Gazette*, **101** (12).

Department of the Environment (1994) *Access to Local Authority and Housing Association Tenancies: a Consultation Paper*, London: DoE.

Department of Health (1992) *Health of the Nation: A Strategy for England and Wales*, London: HMSO.

Department of Health (1994) *Responding to Youth Crime: Findings from Inspections of Youth Justice Sections in Five Local Authority Social Services Departments*, London: HMSO.

Dews, V. and Watts, J. (1995) *Review of Probation Officer Recruitment and Qualifying Training*, London: Home Office.

Dickinson, D. (1994) 'Crime and Unemployment', Faculty of Economics and Politics, University of Cambridge.

Dieskstra, R. (1989) 'Suicide and attempted suicide: an international perspective', *Acta Psychiatrica Scandanavia*, **80**, 1–24.

Dittmar, H. (1992) *The Social Psychology of Material Possessions*, Hemel Hempstead: Harvester Wheatsheaf.

Dominelli, L. and McLeod, E. (1989) *Feminist Social Work*, London: Macmillan.

Dooley, E. (1990) 'Prison suicide in England and Wales', *British Journal of Psychiatry*, **156**, 40–5.

Dorn, N. and South, N. (1987) *A Land Fit For Heroin*, London: Macmillan.

Drakeford, M. (1990) *Credit Unions and Community Economic Development*, Barkingside: Barnardos.

Duster, T. (1995) *Post-Industrialism and Youth Unemployment: A Harbinger for Western Europe*, Washington, DC: Joint Centre for Social and Economic Policy.

Farrington, D.P. (1992) 'Trends in English juvenile delinquency and their explanation', *International Journal of Comparative and Applied Criminal Justice*, **16** (2), 151–63.

Farrington, D.P. and Morris, A.M. (1983) 'Sex, sentencing and reconviction', *British Journal of Criminology*, **26** (4), 229–48.

Farrington, D.P., Gallagher, B., Morley, L., St Ledger, R.J. and West, D. (1986) 'Unemployment, school leaving and crime', *British Journal of Criminology*, **26** (4), 335–56.

Faulkener, D. (1989) 'The future of the probation service: a view from the government', in R. Shaw and R. Haines (eds), *The Criminal Justice System: A Central Role for the Probation Service*, Institute of Criminology: University of Cambridge.

Feest, J. (1988) *Reducing the Prison Population: Lessons from the West German Experience*, London: NACRO.

Field, S. (1990) *Trends in Crime and their Interpretation: A Study of Recorded Crime in Postwar England and Wales*, Home Office Research Study No. 119, London: HMSO.

Fleisher, B.M. (1963) 'The effect of unemployment on juvenile delinquency', *Journal of Political Economy*, **71**, 543–55.

Folkard, M.S., Smith, D.E. and Smith, D.D. (1976) *IMPACT Intensive Matched Probation and After-care Treatment*, Vol. 2, London: HMSO.

Ford, P., Cox, M. and Pritchard, C. (forthcoming, 1995) 'The probation client speaks: towards a redefinition of advise, guide and befriend: a "consumer" survey of probation clients', *Howard Journal of Criminal Justice*.

Foucault, M. (1977) *Discipline and Punish: The Birth of the Prison*, Harmondsworth: Allen Lane.

Franey, R. (1986) *Poor Law*, London: CHAR.

Fulwood, C. (1989) 'Probation, community and inter-agency dimensions: a future look' in R. Shaw and R. Haines (eds), *The Criminal Justice System: A Central Role for the Probation Service*, Institute of Criminology, University of Cambridge.

Gelsthorpe, L. and Raynor, P. (1993) 'The quality of reports prepared in the pilot studies' in J. Bredar (ed.), *Justice Informed*, Vol. II, London: Vera

Institute of Justice.

Gelsthorpe, L. and Raynor, P. (1995) 'Quality and effectiveness in probation officers' reports to sentencers', *British Journal of Criminology*, **35** (2), 188–200.

Gendreau, P. and Ross, R.R. (1979) 'Effective correctional treatment: bibliotherapy for cynics', *Crime and Delinquency*, **25**, 463–89.

Gormally, B., Lyner, O., Mulligan, G. and Warden, M. (1981) *Unemployment and Young Offenders in Northern Ireland*, Belfast: NIACRO.

Gravelle, H.S.E., Hutchinson, G. and Stern, J. (1981) *Mortality and Unemployment: A Cautionary Note*, Discussion Paper No. 95, Centre for Labour Economics, London School of Economics.

Greenberg, D.F. (1977) 'The dynamics of oscillatory punishment processes', *Journal of Criminal Law and Criminology*, **68**, 643–51.

Gunn, J., Madden, A. and Swinton, M. (1991) 'Treatment needs of prisoners with psychiatric disorders', *British Medical Journal*, **303** (6798), 338–41.

Hampshire Probation Service (1992) *Targeting Matrix: A Guide to Structured Decision-making for Practitioners and Sentencers*, Winchester: Hampshire Probation Service.

Harding, J. (1978) *Employment and the Probation and After-Care Service*, Chichester: Barry Rose.

Harding, J. (ed.) (1987) *Probation and the Community*, London: Tavistock.

Harraway, P.C., Brown, A.J., Hignett, C.F., Wilson, C.O., Abbot, J.S., Mortimer, S.A. and Keegan, A.C. (1985) *The Demonstration Unit, 1981–1985*, Inner London Probation Service.

Harris, R.J. (1980) 'A changing service: the case for separating care and control in probation practice', *British Journal of Social Work*, **10** (2), 163–84.

Hayek, F. (1973) *Rules and Order*, London: Routledge and Kegan Paul.

Hayek, F. (1976) *The Mirage of Social Justice*, London: Routledge and Kegan Paul.

Heidensohn, F. (1987) *Women and Crime*, Basingstoke: Macmillan.

Henderson, P. (1987) *Community Work and the Probation Service*, London: National Institute of Social Work.

Hereford and Worcester Probation Service (1982) Report to Staff Conference, unpublished.

Hill, J. (1987) 'Evaluating effectiveness' in J. Harding (ed.), *Probation and the Community*, London: Tavistock.

Holman, B. (1989) *Putting Families First*, London: Macmillan.

Home Office (1978) *A Survey of the South East Prison Population*, Research Bulletin No. 5, 12–24, London: Home Office.

Home Office (1984a) *Criminal Statistics, England and Wales*, London: HMSO.

Home Office (1984b) *Probation Service in England and Wales: Statement of National Objectives and Priorities*, London: Home Office.

Home Office (1988a) *Punishment, Custody and the Community*, London: HMSO.

Home Office (1988b) *Review of Non-custodial Offender Accommodation*, Circular No. 35/1988, London: Home Office.

Home Office (1990) *Supervision and Punishment in the Community: A Framework for Action*, London: HMSO.

Home Office (1992) *National Standards*, London: Home Office.

Home Office (1993a) *Bail Information: Report of a Thematic Inspection*, London: HM Inspectorate of Probation.

Home Office (1993b) *Monitoring of the Criminal Justice Act 1991 – Data from a Special Data Collection Exercise*, Statistical Bulletin 25/93, London: Home Office.

Home Office (1994a) *Cautions, Court Proceedings and Sentencing: England and Wales 1993*, Statistical Bulletin 19/94, London: Home Office Research and Statistics Dept.

Home Office (1994b) *Youth Offenders and the Probation Service: A Report of H.M. Inspectorate of Probation Thematic Inspection*, London: HMSO.

Home Office (1995a) *Review of Probation Officer Recruitment and Qualifying Training: Discussion Paper*, London: Home Office.

Home Office (1995b) *Strengthening Punishment in the Community*, Cm. 2780, London: HMSO.

Home Office (1995c) *National Standards*, London: Home Office.

Homewood, R. (1989) 'Must the poor pay more? Wigan's community credit union', *Probation Journal*, **36** (4), 159–64.

Hood, R. and Cordovil, G. (1992) *Race and Sentencing*, Oxford: Clarendon Press.

Hope, T. and Shaw, M. (eds) (1988) *Communities and Crime Reductions*, London: HMSO.

Hucklesby, A. (1994) 'The use and abuse of conditional bail', *Howard Journal*, **33** (3), 258–70.

Hudson, B. (1989) 'Discrimination and disparity: the influence of race on sentencing', *New Community*, **16** (1), 23–34.

Hudson, B.A. (1993) *Penal Policy and Social Justice*, London: Macmillan.

Hudson, B., Roberts, C. and Cullen, R. (1993) *Training for Training with Mentally Disordered Offenders*, London, CCETSW.

Hughes, J. (1991) *Poverty and Offending in Somerset: An Analysis of Data Collected from Social Enquiry Reports*, Somerset Probation Service.

Hutchinson-Reis, M. (1986) 'After the uprising – social work on Broadwater Farm', *Critical Social Policy*, **6** (2), 70–9.

Huxley, P., Korer, J.R. and Tolley, S. (1987) 'The psychiatric caissons of clients referred to an urban social services department', *British Journal of Social Work*, **17** (5), 507–21.

Inner London Probation Service (1991) *Report of the Poverty Task Group*, ILPS.

James, A. and Bottomley, A.K. (1994) 'Probation partnerships revisited', *Howard Journal*, **33** (2), 158–68.

Jeffs, M. and Smith, R. (1994) 'Young people, youth and a new authoritarianism', *Youth and Policy*, Autumn, **46**, 17–32.

Jenkins, J. and Lawrence, D. (1992) 'Black groups initiative review', unpublished paper, Inner London Probation Service.

Jones, M., Mordecai, M.M., Rutter, F. and Thomas, L. (1991) 'The Miskin model of group work with women offenders', *Groupwork*, **4**, 215–30.

Jordan, B. (1987) *Rethinking Welfare*, Oxford: Blackwell.

Jordan, B. (1989) *The Common Good: Citizenship, Morality and Self-Interest*, Oxford: Blackwell.

Jordan, B. (1990) *Social Work in an Unjust Society*, Hemel Hempstead: Harvester Wheatsheaf.

Jordan, B. (1992) 'Authoritarian Benthamism', in P. Senior and B. Williams (eds), *Probation Practice after the Criminal Justice Act, 1991*, Sheffield: PAVIC.

Jordan, B. and Jones, M. (1988) 'Poverty, the underclass and probation practice', *Probation Journal*, **35** (4), 123–7.

Jordan, B. and Redley, M. (1994) 'Polarisation, underclass and the welfare state', *Work, Employment and Society*, **8** (2), 153–76.

Jordan, B., James, S., Kay, H. and Redley, M. (1992) *Trapped in Poverty? Labour Market Decisions in Low-Income Households*, London: Routledge.

Knapman, E. (1982) Unpublished MSc thesis, Cranfield Institute of Technology.

Leonard, P. (1975) 'Towards a paradigm for radical practice' in R. Bailey and M. Brake (eds), *Radical Social Work*, London: Edward Arnold.

Lloyd, A. (1989) 'Aiding and abetting the faults in the structure', *Probation Journal*, **36** (1), 22–5.

Lowe, R. (1993) *The Welfare State in Britain since 1945*, London: Macmillan.

Luckhaus, L. (1982) 'A plea for PMT in the criminal law' in Susan Edwards (ed.), *Gender Sex and the Law*, London: Croom Helm.

Lyons, B. (1992) 'Game theory' in S. Hargreaves Heap, M. Hollis, B. Lyons, R. Sugden and A. Weale (eds), *The Theory of Choice: A Critical Guide*, Oxford: Blackwell.

McIvor, G. (1991) 'Social work intervention in community service', *British Journal of Social Work*, **21**, 591–609.

McWilliams, W. (1987) 'Probation, pragmatism and policy', *Howard Journal*, **26** (2), 97–121.

Marklund, S. (1992) 'The decomposition of social policy in Sweden', *Scandinavian Journal of Social Welfare*, **1** (1), 2–11.

Martin, J.P. (1962) *Offenders as Employees*, London: Macmillan.

Martin, J.P. and Webster, W. (1971) *Social Consequences of Conviction*, London: Heinemann.

Martinson, R. (1974) 'What works?', *The Public Interest*, March, 22–54.

Mead, L. (1986) *Beyond Entitlement: The Social Obligations of Citizenship*, New York: Basic Books.

Merseyside Probation Service (1994) *A Report on the South Section Drugs Team.*

Minford, P. (1984) 'State expenditure: a study in waste', Supplement to *Economic Affairs,* **4** (3).

Morris, A. and Gelsthorpe, L. (1990) 'Can't pay or won't pay?' *The Magistrate,* October, 170/71.

Morris, P. and Beverley, F. (1975) *On Licence: A Study of Parole,* London: Wiley.

Mott, J. (1989) *Reducing Heroin Related Crime,* Research Bulletin No. 26, 30–33, London: Home Office Research and Planning Unit.

Murray, C. (1984) *Losing Ground: American Social Policy, 1950–1980,* New York: Basic Books.

Murray, C. (1990) *Britain's Emerging Underclass,* London: Institute of Economic Affairs.

NACRO (1993) *Annual Report, 1992–93,* London: NACRO.

NACRO (1994) *Prison Overcrowding – Recent Developments,* London: NACRO.

Naffine, N. and Gale, F. (1989) 'Testing the nexus: crime, gender and unemployment', *British Journal of Criminology,* **29** (2), 144–56.

National Association of Probation Officers (1985) *Housing Practice in the Probation Service,* Social Policy Committee, London: NAPO.

National Association of Probation Officers (1988) *Dealing with the Social Fund,* Professional Practice Committee, London: NAPO.

National Association of Probation Officers (1993) *Probation Caseload: Income and Employment. A Study of the Financial Circumstances of 1331 Offenders on Probation Supervision,* London: NAPO.

National Association of Probation Officers (1994a) *Benefits System Discriminates Against Offenders and their Families,* London: NAPO.

National Association of Probation Officers (1994b) *Fines and Debtors' Goal: A Briefing Paper,* London: NAPO.

Nellis, M. (1995) 'Probation values for the 1990s', *Howard Journal,* **34** (1), 19–44.

Newman, O. (1981) *The Challenge of Corporatism,* London: Macmillan.

North, J., Adair, H., Langley, B., Mills, J. and Morten, G. (1992) *The Dog that Finally Barked: The Tyneside Disturbances of 1991, a Probation Perspective,* Northumbria Probation Service.

Northumbria Probation Service (1994) *Survey of Probation Practice on Poverty Issues,* Northumbria Probation Service.

Nottinghamshire Probation Service (1990) *Young Offenders Alone: A Survey of the Personal Circumstances of Young Offenders Living Away From Home in Nottingham,* Nottinghamshire Probation Service.

Offe, C. and Preuss, U.K. (1990) 'Democratic institutions and moral resources', in D. Held (ed.), *Political Theory Today,* Cambridge: Polity.

Parker, H. (1982) *The Moral Hazard of Social Insurance,* London: Institute of Economic Affairs.

Parker, H. (1989) *Instead of the Dole: An Enquiry into Tax-Benefit Integration*, London: Routledge.

Parton, N. (1994) '"Problematics of Government", (Post)-Modernity and social work', *British Journal of Social Work*, **24** (1), 9–32.

Paylor, I. (1992) *Homelessness and Ex-Offenders: A Case For Reform*, Social Work Monograph, University of East Anglia, Norwich.

Pearson, G. (1989) 'Women and men without work: the political economy is personal', in C. Rojek, G. Peacock and C. Stewart (eds), *The Haunt of Misery*, London: Routledge.

Peelo, M., Stewart, J., Stewart, G. and Prior, A. (1992) *A Sense of Justice: Offenders as Victims of Crime*, London: Association of Chief Officers of Probation.

Perkins, E., Roberts, S. and Moore, N. (1992) *Helping Clients Claim Their Benefits: Information Needs of Informal Policy Advisors*, London: Policy Studies Institute.

Pincus, A. and Minahan, A. (1973) *Social Work Practice: Model and Method*, Itasca: F.E. Peacock.

Pitts, J. (1992) 'The end of an era', *Howard Journal*, **31** (2), 133–49.

Priestley, P., McGuire, J., Flegg, D., Hemsley, V. and Welham, D. (1978) *Social Skills and Personal Problem Solving: A Handbook of Methods*, London, Tavistock.

Pritchard, C. (1992) 'Is there a link between unemployment and suicide in young men? A UK comparison with other countries of the European Community', *British Journal of Psychiatry*, **160**, 750–6.

Pritchard, C. and Clooney, D. (1994) *Single Homelessness: Fractured Lives and Fragmented Policies*, Report to Department of Environment, Bournemouth Churches Housing Association.

Pritchard, C. and Cox, M. (forthcoming) 'Young Adults at Risk of HIV Infection: A further consequence of the "Cycle of Deprivation?"', *Research Policy and Planning*.

Pritchard, C., Cotton, A., Godson, D., Cox, M. and Weeks, S. (1992) 'Mental illness, drug and alcohol misuse and HIV risk behaviour in 214 young adult (18–35 year) probation clients: implications for policy practice and training', *Social Work and Social Sciences Review*, **3** (3), 227–42.

Purser, R. (1987) 'The drink/drug offender', in J. Harding (ed.), *Probation and the Community*, London: Tavistock.

Raynor, P. (1991) 'Sentencing with and without reports', *Howard Journal*, **30** (4), 293–300.

Raynor, P. and Vanstone, M. (1993) 'Straight thinking on probation, effectiveness and the non-treatment paradigm', paper given to the British Criminology Conference, July 1993.

Raynor, P., Smith, D. and Vanstone, M. (1994) *Effective Probation Practice*, London: Macmillan.

Rieple, A. and Harper, M. (1993) 'Ex-offenders and enterprise', *Howard Journal*, **32** (4), 271–5.

Ross, P.R. and Fabiano, E.A. (1985) *Time To Think: A Cognitive Model of Delinquency Prevention and Offender Rehabilitation*, Johnson City, Academy of Arts and Science.

Rowntree Foundation (1990) *The Contribution of the Social Fund to Relieving Poverty*, Social Policy Research Findings No. 8, York.

Shepherd, D. (1990) 'Mentally disordered offenders and the Probation Service', unpublished paper given to the Department of Social Work Studies, University of Southampton.

Smith, D., Paylor, I. and Mitchell, P. (1993) 'Partnerships between the independent sector and the probation service', *Howard Journal*, **32**, 25–39.

South Glamorgan County Council (1994) *Director of Social Services Report on Existing County Council Services*, Cardiff: South Glamorgan County Council.

Stewart, G. and Stewart, J. (1991) *Relieving Poverty? Use of the Social Fund by Social Work Clients and Other Agencies*, London: Association of Metropolitan Authorities.

Stewart, G. and Stewart, J. (1993a) *Social Circumstances Of Younger Offenders Under Probation Supervision*, London: Association of Chief Officers of Probation.

Stewart, G. and Stewart, J. (1993b) *Social Work and Housing*, London: Macmillan.

Stewart, G., Lee, R. and Stewart, J. (1986) 'The right approach to social security: the case of the board and lodging regulations', *Journal of Law and Society*, **13** (3), 371–99.

Stewart, G., Stewart, J., Prior, A. and Peelo, M. (1989) *Surviving Poverty: Probation Work and Benefits Policy*, Wakefield: Association of Chief Officers of Probation.

Stewart, J., Smith, D.B., Stewart, G. and Fullwood, C. (1994) *Understanding Offending Behaviour*, London: Longman.

Stockley, D., Canter, D. and Bishop, D. (1993) *Young People on the Move*, Department of Psychology, University of Surrey.

Stone, C. (1989) *Public Interest Case Assessment: Final Report of the Probation Initiative 'Diversion from Custody and Prosecution'*, New York: Vera Institute of Justice.

Sviridoff, M. and McElroy, J. (1985) *Employment and Crime: A Summary Report*, London and New York: Vera Institute of Justice.

Tarling, R. (1982) *Unemployment and Crime*, Research Bulletin No. 14, London: Home Office Research and Planning Unit.

Taylor, D. (1986) 'Summary of the Results in the Humberside Probation Client Caseload Survey' in M. Backhouse, I. Gurevitch and S. Silver (eds), *Problem Drinkers and the Statutory Services*, Hull: Humberside Probation Service.

Thomas, P.A. and Costigan, R.S. (1992) 'Health care or punishment?: Prisoners with HIV/AIDS', *Howard Journal*, **31** (4), 321–36.

Thorpe, D.H., Smith, D., Green, C.J. and Paley, J. (1980) *Out of Care: The Community Support of Juvenile Offenders*, London: Allen and Unwin.

Tonak, D. (1992) *Public Interest Case Assessment*. Volume Two of the Final Report on the Probation Initiative 'Diversion from custody and prosecution', New York: Vera Institute of Justice.

Townsend, T. and Davidson, N. (1982) *Inequalities in Health*, Harmondsworth: Penguin.

Training Agency (1989) *Prisoners Into Jobs*.

Tutt, N. (ed.) (1978) *Alternative Strategies for Coping with Crime*, Oxford: Blackwell.

UNSDRI (1976) *Economic Crises and Crime*, Rome: United Nations Social Defence Research Institute.

Vagg, J. (1992) 'A little local difficulty: The management of difficult to place people', *International Journal of Law and Psychiatry*, **15** (2), 129–38.

Van Parijs, P. (1992) *Arguing for Basic Income: Ethical Foundations for a Radical Reform*, London: Verso.

Vanstone, M. (1994) *A Moral Good Examined: A Survey of the Standard Probation Order in Mid Glamorgan*, Department of Applied Social Studies, Swansea University.

Verboud, Michael and Padel, Una (1992) 'In Her Majesty's Prisons', *Le Journal du Sida* (English edn).

Walker, C. (1994) *Managing Poverty: The Limits of Social Assistance*, London: Routledge.

Walmsley, R., Howard, L. and White, S. (1992) *The National Prison Survey: Main Findings*, Home Office Research Study No. 128, London: HMSO.

Welsh Office (1993) *Juvenile Remands in Wales: A Social Services Inspectorate Survey of Policy and Practice Relating to Pre-Court and Pre-Sentence Services*, Cardiff: Welsh Office.

Whitehead, M. (1990) *The Health Divide: Inequalities in Health in the 1980s*, Harmondsworth: Penguin.

Williams, B. (1991) 'Probation contact with long-term prisoners', *Probation Journal*, **38** (1), 4–9.

Williams, B. (1994) 'Probation training in the UK: from charity organisation to jobs for the boys', *Social Work Education*, **13** (3), 99–108.

Wilson, H. (1987) 'Parental supervision re-examined', *British Journal of Criminology*, **27** (3), 275–301.

Woolf, H. (1991) *Prison Disturbances, April 1990*, Cmnd 1456, London: HMSO.

Zimring, F.E. and Hawkins, G. (1994) 'The growth of imprisonment in California', *British Journal of Criminology*, **34**, 83–96.

Index

Advocacy Skills

A HANDBOOK FOR HUMAN SERVICE PROFESSIONALS

Neil Bateman

Advocacy is a skill used by many people in human service organisations. Social workers, community medical staff and advice workers are a few who will use such skills. Advocacy is used to overcome obstacles and to secure tangible results for customers – extra money, better services and housing. Neil Bateman's book sets out a model for effective professional practice, and outlines a number of approaches to advocacy.

This is a seminal work; no other book has been published in the UK which explains how advocacy skills can be used and developed. Advocacy is becoming part of the everyday work of many people. Advocacy Skills will be a valuable handbook for anyone concerned with the rights of others.

Neil Bateman is currently a Principal Officer with Suffolk County Council, an adviser to the Association of County Councils and a visiting lecturer at the University of East Anglia.

1995   176 pages   1 85742 200 7   £14.95

Price subject to change without notification

arena

— *The* —
LEGAL RIGHTS
Manual
SECOND EDITION
A guide for social workers and advice centres

Jeremy Cooper

This book provides social workers, advice centres and those engaged in caring for others, together with their clients, with an up-to-date body of information and advice on their legal rights, covering a wide range of areas and activities.

Written in a concise, non-technical and readable style the book describes how individuals and groups can use the law to their advantage in a diverse range of settings, including: housing, the workplace; living with mental or physical disability, dealing with council and other public officials, problems with the police, living with old age, and as a consumer of goods and services. It also provides the reader with a mass of information on where to go for further advice and assistance in each of these areas. This fully updated and revised second edition states the law as it stands on 1 March 1994.

Jeremy Cooper is a barrister and Professor of Law and Head of the Law Division at the Southampton Institute.

1994   **319 pages**   **1 85742 136 1**   **£19.95**

Price subject to change without notification

arena

The Police and Social Workers

Second Edition

Terry Thomas

Social workers and police officers are in daily contact with one another in various areas of their work. This book offers a clear guide to that inter-agency work and critically examines how it is carried out in practice.

This second edition of the book has been substantially revised to take account of changes in the law, policy and procedures affecting both police and social workers. In particular the Children Act 1989, The Criminal Justice Act 1991 and the findings of the Royal Commission on Criminal Justice 1993. The opportunity has also been taken to revise parts of the original text to ensure as clear a light as possible is thrown on police-social work collaboration – illustrating both the positive and the negative.

Terry Thomas is Senior Lecturer in Social Work at Leeds Metropolitan University.

1994   **346 pages**   **1 85742 157 4**   **£14.95**

Price subject to change without notification

How the Law Thinks About Children

SECOND EDITION

Michael King and Christine Piper

"A minor classic... it stimulates and advances our understanding of the relationship between law and science, and law and children." Professor Michael Freeman, British Journal of Criminology of the first edition

How the Law Thinks About Children considers the ways in which legal systems deal with issues of child abuse, child custody and juvenile delinquency by constructing their own 'realities'. It offers many original insights into the relationship between law and child welfare science and provides a critical analysis of decision making about children welfare in several different countries. It concludes by pointing the way to a new era of 'child responsiveness' for courts dealing with issues involving children. The first edition of this book has been widely recognized as a milestone in sociological analysis of the legal system's role in regulating children and families. This completely revised second edition clarifies and develops several of the theoretical issues that so intrigued readers of the earlier version.

Michael King and **Christine Piper** are Co-Directors of The Centre for the Study of Law, the Child and the Family, Brunel University.

1995   207 pages   1 85742 226 0   £16.95

Price subject to change without notification

arena

LAW for
SOCIAL WORKERS:
An Introduction
2ND EDITION
Caroline Ball

The second edition of this book provides a basic introduction, for those with little knowledge of law and the legal system, to the legal context of social work with different client groups. The Children Act 1989 has come into force since publication of the first edition of this book, and the section on children and families reflects the radical changes which have resulted. An outline of the law relating to mental health, housing, education, the criminal process and young offenders similarly reflects the impact of the National Health Service and Community Care Act 1990 and the Criminal Justice Act 1991, on work with other client groups.

Probation officers and local authority social workers require a sound and basic competence in the application of law at the time of qualification, which needs reinforcing and updating throughout professional practice. This book will aid both the acquisition and the development of the knowledge base necessary for competence.

Caroline Ball is Lecturer in Law at the School of Social Work, University of East Anglia.

1992   140 pages   1 85742 067 5   £8.95

Price subject to change without notification

arena

CONCISE GUIDE TO

Customs of Minority Ethnic Religions

David Collins
Manju Tank
Abdul Basith

Much has been written on the subject of Community Relations. This small book does not claim to add to this knowledge, but rather to distil it in a brief, orderly, and accessible form for the everyday reader, who needs basic guidance for the purposes of everyday work. It makes no assumptions about existing understanding or interest on the part of the reader, and aims to enable readers to meet the needs of minority ethnic consumers in a more sensitive and respectful way.

The Guide contains basic useful information on Judaism, Sikhism, Hinduism, Islam, Buddhism/Taoism/Confucianism, and Rastafarianism. Each section is divided into modules dealing with Symbols, Languages and Scripts, Names, Beliefs, Prayer, Religious Festivals, Dress, Diet, Medical Treatment, Social Rules, Birth Customs and Visiting.

1993   84 pages   1 85742 120 5   £5.50

Price subject to change without notification

arena